CMYK:

THE PROCESS OF LIFE TOGETHER

CMYK:

THE PROCESS OF LIFE TOGETHER

Justin McRoberts

CMYK: The Process of Life Together

Copyright © 2013 Justin McRoberts

Five Foot Six and a Half Music (ASCAP)

"The more genuine and the deeper our community becomes, the more will everything else between us recede, the more clearly and purely will Jesus Christ and His work become the one and only thing that is vital between us."

-Dietrich Bonhoeffer, Life Together

TABLE OF CONTENTS

Foreword by Mark Labberton
Introduction

PART ONE: C

PART TWO: M

PART THREE: Y

Foreword

Biblical faith and raw life are a rare combination. Various fears are among the reasons: the fear of disappointing or misrepresenting God; the fear of doubt, the fear of the messiness of life, the fear of inadequacy, the fear of being wrong, the fear of not belonging, the fear of being known, the fear of the unknown, the fear of being human, the fear of pain, the fear of our bodies or of our emotions or of our reason. The list could go on.

The way this shows itself is when the church refers to human neediness but leaves the impression that the needs are "out there," not right here; or that those needs are "back then," not right now. It shows up when the church quiets human grief or doubt or rage with a blanket of faith-talk, rather than with open confession and true lament. It happens when the people of God forget that we walk by faith and not by sight, and lose track of the affirmation that we see through a glass darkly—*at best*. Christians talk about faith as a pathway to life, but the impression is that it is more like a prophylactic from life.

The ironic tragedy that comes from this disjunction between faith and candor is that it leaves the impression that perhaps the God of the Bible, if there is such a God, needs to be protected, or at least kept distant, from the very people this

God supposedly loves. It is as though God and raw life don't mix or can't touch. No wonder such a God would have little meaning or value in a raw world. When Christian people choose the cleaner option of keeping God and raw life apart, the incarnation, death, and resurrection of Jesus Christ becomes a religious cartoon.

At its best, the community of God's people is meant to be among the most tangible evidences that God and raw life come together. This, however, is one of the least apparent inferences one might draw from the witness of the church. Experience of true, honest, sustained community in, with, and for life's realities is costly. It means facing our own raw need, as well as that of others, and a great deal of life is spent trying to do anything but these two things.

The gift of this CMYK Project is that it brings this rare combination together. Any who have known Justin McRoberts would be surprised if it did not do so, of course. The blend is Justin's life and vocation. It has been evident in his music and leadership for many years. But here it is exposed vividly. So are many relationships and the quest for community through life over time. What we are given is an invitation to join Justin in an unfinished, honest, empathic, hurting story of hope. That is why the story must be told in many dimensions: the letters, the lyrics and music, the visual art, the interviews. This is not an invitation into a cartoon encounter with God, nor with each other. It is a multi-dimensional, littered, vivid, living story of being human, seeking God and neighbor.

The reason this invitation can be offered at all is not that Justin is remarkable and eccentric (which he is). The reason is that the God Justin testifies to in Jesus Christ has made human beings for this courageous, awkward journey, where the fully divine and the truly human meet. This is life's most breath-taking possibility, and as Justin so movingly illustrates, we may find it is like laying hold of the third rail. No one should find it comfortable.

-Mark Labberton
Author of "The Dangerous Act Of Loving Your Neighbor"

Introduction

A Word About Letters

I once wrote a letter on a yellow rubber duck. I then stamped the duck and mailed him to Tacoma, Washington, where he was received by the clever and beautiful Art Major I had fallen for. That duck was just one in a series of items I sent north by mail during the years Amy and I dated. From 1996, when we met, until we were married in 1999, we exchanged letters of one sort or another, almost weekly. We still have most of those letters in boxes. But the letters we remember best are the ones that don't fit in boxes, like that rubber duck. We wrote letters on beach balls, eggs, road signs, orange pylons, spoons, bananas, etc... Amy once wrote a note on the underside of a frisbee, stamped the top of it and sent it. The frisbee read "Nice Catch!" followed by a list of things we planned to do when we lived in the same town. In turn, I sent the sole of a hiking boot that had fallen out the back of my busted-up kicks during a hike. I stamped the unpleasant thing and sent it to her (without an envelope) bearing a note that read, "Here... you can have my sole."

Yes, that's gross. I know.
But it's gross in a charming kind of way.
And it worked.
She married me.

Amy and I didn't live in the same town until after our wedding. And while our long-distance courtship might not seem too big a deal with Facebook, Twitter and smartphones weighing heavily in today's social tool-belt, what if I told you that I lived without a Facebook profile, didn't own a computer and that neither Amy or I had a cell phone. What we had were the words we exchanged through the mail and the artifacts on which they were written. Getting to know one another that way meant that those letters, most of them written by hand, said at least as much in form as they did in content. Before the card (or the box of Golden Grahams) read "I miss you" or "here is what I'm up to" or "please get a real job so that when we get married we can eat regularly," it said, "You are worth the effort to write this all down, buy some stamps and convince the post-office clerk to send it through." When communication theorist Marshall McLuhan coined the phrase "the medium is the message," he paved way for a long distance courtship wherein "the rubber duck is the romance."

In similar fashion, this project (the book you're holding and the music that accompanies it) was inspired by a letter. Not an essay written about things I found pertinent or a song with which I resonated. It was a letter written directly to me. I find there to be a powerful difference between reading generally about a topic and reading words written to me about the particular life I'm living. That's part of why I find it so important that the New Testament is made up almost entirely of letters. Paul never sat down to write an essay on the philosophical implications of the Incarnation. He wrote letters to particular groups of people in particular places for which knowledge of the Incarnation was key to their process of life together. It seems to me that Paul's impetus for writing those letters was not that he knew a thing or two about Jesus, but that he knew people in Corinth and Ephesus who were learning to follow Jesus and knew that his voice could be a key in their process.

In early 2010, I started writing a series of songs and letters that eventually would become the heart of this book. The vast majority of those songs and letters have been written for people who know me as a pastor more than as an artist. And while the project strays beyond that boundary at times, relational proximity remains its dominant characteristic. So, while these letters, lyrics, essays and interviews may touch on themes that are Universal that is not my aim. There are many insightful and qualified women and men writing books and lecturing on the topics weaved throughout this work: faith and doubt, community and individuality, sexuality and identity, hope and loss. And while I can't be sure what my voice adds to the conversation in that sphere, I am convinced that I can help add clarity to the lives of people I know who are touched by those topics. For my part, the most powerful voices in my life have seldom been voices of people well versed in the issues I face. Most often they have been voices of friends well versed in my life — friends who see the issues I face as elements in my process rather than my defining properties. Likewise, I'm not expertly trained to deal with the all the various issues my loved ones face, but I am familiar enough with the lives those issues are part of to provide clarity, context and guidance.

A Word About Colors

There are three magazines on the table next to me. Nearest to me is the November issue of WIRED, featuring late night talk show host Jimmy Fallon. Next to that is the October Sports Illustrated bearing the image of Detroit Tigers first baseman Miguel Cabrera. Furthest from me is Image Journal #72 donning an untitled oil piece by late visual artist Guy Chase. The images on the covers of these periodicals have very little in common. The subject matter, layout and design of these three periodicals are different in all ways but one: each is made up of the CMYK printing process. CMYK refers to the four inks used in color printing: Cyan, Magenta, Yellow and Key (black). Ink is applied in tiny, overlapping dots at varying percentages of saturation. This is called "half-toning." When the primary colors Cyan, Magenta and Yellow are combined, they result in secondary colors like red, green and blue. With half-toning and the addition of black or "Key," any color can be printed. I know you didn't plan on getting a color process lesson but I find this whole process intriguing. So much so that I named this project after the CMYK print process.

The four basic colors of the CMYK print process fundamentally need one another. If the there were no colors but magenta, there would no longer be "Magenta." Magenta needs to be in relationship with colors that are not magenta in order to be Magenta. In short, Magenta is Magenta because nothing else is. Likewise with Cyan, Yellow and Black. In other words, each color's identity is established in its relationship with and proximity to other colors. This inspires me.

When the CMYK print process is done correctly, the Cyan, Magenta and Yellow plates are "Keyed" to the black plate, which is where the black plate gets its name, "K." What this means to me is that while black is only one element of the process it is the key element. Without black, a printed image would not have a full-range of color and the clarity and depth of that image would be lost. This encourages me.

I have to look closely at an image over a period of time before I can see what it is essentially made up of. The casual glance is never enough. This challenges me. These themes emerged in me thinking about the CMYK print process and deeply informed this work:

—The necessary role of **relationship** in the formation of identity.

—The essential role of **darkness** in finding clarity.

—The basic **commonality** of seemingly incompatible images.

I see powerful and enlightening parallels between the CMYK print process and the process of life together.

A Word About Reading This Book

In the same way we originally released the CMYK songs on separate EP's entitled C, M and Y, we have divided this book into three main sections entitled C, M and Y. Those sections are further divided into letters, lyrics and personal reflections. There is no correct sequence in which to read the book though I would strongly suggest reading the actual text of each piece from left to right. (If that is not your method I would like to know how you got this far already!)

Finally, I humbly suggest becoming familiar with the musical element of CMYK. I made the project to work cohesively and believe it is most fully engaged that way. Along with the original three EP's mentioned above, I have also produced an album entitled, "K." I selected key songs from each EP and made fully re-imagined recordings of them. Those songs were then weaved together with recordings of traditional songs we felt resonated strongly with the existing content. You can find the music on iTunes or JustinMcRoberts.com.

PART ONE: C

They Don't Mean
What They Used To

"There is a knowledge that is only arrived at by fighting for
what I believe to be true and right.... and losing."

I had a brief and life-altering conversation with a young pastor who had recently assumed leadership of the church his father previously pastored. Only a few months before that conversation he and his wife lost their daughter in a regrettable accident. That conversation set a much needed part of my process in motion; one in which I would learn to connect with God as a person.

Letter To A Young Pastor

You invited me to your hometown to play songs and tell stories for the people in your church. Before the event, you told me about losing your eight-month-old daughter and asked if I would write a song for you and your wife. It has been over seven years since then and only recently have I found the language to do what you asked of me. Ironically, after all these years, the language I found most appropriate was yours. And it is language that requires a level of courage I still find challenging.

Though I held in common with you the pain of losing loved ones, I couldn't imagine losing a child, much less know how to approach such a thing in song. But it wasn't only the unsettling and disorienting nature of your story that made it difficult to respond. The larger part of my reticence had to do with the posture I had been living in as a Christian and an artist. Up to that point, I was most often writing songs and stories in an effort to explain and teach. I was using my art to wrap things up. When you asked me to write a song for you, I took that to mean that I should write something that would make your story somehow more understandable or even palatable. I felt the challenge to explain it or point toward some kind of resolution. But you weren't asking me to explain anything. Nor were you asking me to resolve anything. What you were asking for was language that might help describe and clarify that dark moment in your process exactly as it was and know that it was all right to be there. But music had become a form of control for me; a way to manage my life and world. I've since learned (in part due to our conversation) that while teaching and instruction are good purposes for art, they are not all of what art can or even ought to be.

More than seven years later, I was able to hear more clearly what you were asking of me. More importantly, I could hear what you were saying about your own process. I remember you saying that you believed all the things you had always believed about God but that those things didn't mean what they used to.

You believed God is loving. But that did not mean he always provided in the way you wanted.

You believed God is good. But that did not mean God's design matched your hopes.

You believed God is faithful. But that did not mean God always protected young children from the harms of the world.

Then you said something that truly floored me. You said God had the right to do or allow whatever God chose to do or allow, but that didn't mean that you had to agree with Him about it.

Disagree with God?
You could do that?
You could say, "I know You are God and I am not. But I am not at all happy with what You have done here"?

At the time, this all seemed so dangerous and personal. I was uncomfortable with such thoughts. But hadn't we been taught that God is accessible, personal and dangerous? Wasn't that what we invited others to believe? What you shared with me was a much fuller expression of that truth than I had previously heard. I believed that I could have more than just a general knowledge of God's existence. I believed that I could have a living relationship with the Creator. But what you said about your tragedy led me to see that one of the hallmarks of every healthy, honest, serious relationship is the freedom and ability to disagree.

Witnessing your courage to openly disagree with God was one of the moments in my process that began a richer, more nuanced, more human practice of faith. Your story shook me and in doing so, it shook the dust off an old image of God I was holding onto; one in which God was a Thing or an Idea I could have some knowledge of rather than the Person who had invited me into an active relationship. You were asking me to help you in a moment in your life's process for which you lacked language; a moment marked by conflict and disagreement. As it turned out, I lacked that language as well and ultimately found it in the things you said.

May your continued courage help to set free those you teach and lead. May they follow you in living a richer, more vibrant relationship with God, who has revealed Himself to us in the Person of Christ, the Lord.

Lyrics: They Don't Mean What They Used To

I'll sing these songs for you
But they don't mean quite what they used to
I'll sing these words to you
But only really cuz I'm supposed to

Her absence is a presence
Far more tangible than yours
Her silence has a volume
So much louder than your voice

You give me words to read
And yet my eyes are tired of reading
Light by which I can see
And yet I've grown so tired of seeing

Her life my greatest blessing
And yet you give and take away
So as I gave I take away my praise

Cuz I can't stop thinking about it
I won't stop thinking about it

And so I run to you
If only to tell you that I'm leaving
What hope I've left in you
Is that you'll finally hear me screaming

Cuz I can't stop thinking about you
I won't stop thinking about you

Reflection: Chutzpah

In sixth grade I had a pair of friends who fought after school, at the bike racks, just about once a month. Their names were Matt and Mike. I don't remember why they started fighting in the first place. As likely as anything, they had some disagreement about the actual sequence of the "up, down, left, right, A + B" Nintendo controller cheat. For the record, I believe it was Up, Up, Down, Down, Left, Right, Left, Right, A, B, Select and then Start. If you believe it to be otherwise, you know where to meet me and when.*

Matt and Mike's fights were never particularly violent events. There was usually a lot of pushing, grabbing, name-calling and some general thrashing about, as if both of them were contesting with the same swarm of invisible bees. It would almost always end with someone in a headlock. Well, not just someone; it was always Matt. To the best of my recollection, Matt lost every one of those fights, without exception. I also recall that after every loss, Matt would adamantly claim that he had not fought his hardest and would then, on the heels of that admission, challenge Mike to yet another fight, after school, at the bike racks... which he would again lose and again claim that he hadn't fought his hardest, and so on. Eventually it got boring and the crowd of on-lookers shrunk since we all knew the sad ending. Regardless, Matt and Mike went right on duking it out,

* *bike racks, after school*

month after month. Which meant that so did Matt's protestation that "I didn't fight my hardest."

In my experience, many of our fights with God have a similar tone; we hold something back and walk away frustrated. Friends of mine carry deep resentments towards God because of things they believe God has done or things they think God should have done but didn't. I'm convinced that these resentments often last far longer than they need to. But because we haven't honestly and completely aired our grievance, pain or complaint, the tension just builds quietly under our skin. Maybe we figure that questioning God is a losing battle or that our complaint is too small a thing for God to concern Himself with. Whatever the reason, I think that when we hold our grievances inward, God's "goodness and love" become Ideas we begrudgingly agree to, like a math equation. In doing this, we eventually settle for an unsettled and distant 'belief' in God rather than a living, vibrant, active and complex relationship. My interpretation of the events that cause me grief might be wrong or they might be right but I can never truly know if I do not fully voice my complaint to God. I have come to believe that there is a faith that only comes by way of fighting tooth and nail for what I believe to be true and right... and losing. Such faith requires "chutzpah." Chutzpah is a derivative of an old Yiddish word meaning "audacity." In practice, chutzpah means having the guts to say to God "I disagree." It's not a thing found frequently in the Bible but there is certainly precedent for it and I firmly believe that it is part of a healthy faith process. I see chutzpah in a few of the Psalms and the Lamentations of Jeremiah but most prominently in the story of Job. Job railed against God, calling Him unfair and unjust. In the end, Job's conceptions of fairness and justice were transformed in the light of a broader, deeper and more comprehensive knowledge of God; a knowledge come to by way of losing that fight. Part of what Job's story has done for me is frame the relationship between God and His people in more relational terms — seeing God as a Person to whom I can complain, even when my complaint is against Him.

I am not suggesting we bemoan every scrape and bruise. I know that not all injustice is equal. What I am suggesting is a process of faith in which, when something sincerely hurts or when life really does stop making sense, we carry our complaint to God like we would carry an offering; we sit in protest before Him just as we would in sit in reverence. We plead and we cry and we shout and pace, just as we would pray and praise and sing and dance. We return over and over until either the mountain has moved or our hearts have changed.

During the first season of the "West Wing," the President's Chief of Staff, Leo McGarry, gathers the White House staff into his office for an impromptu meeting. They have been trying to push through legislation they believed in and have been shut down for the umpteenth time. Noting that his staff had grown weary and were starting to pull their punches, Leo doesn't hold a strategy session to figure out ways around the political obstacles in front of them. Instead, he challenges his team, saying "If we're gonna walk into walls, I want us running into 'em full speed." His challenge is to shift their focus from winning or losing battles to fighting those battles in such a way as reflects their seriousness. "We're gonna lose some of these," he goes on "but we're going to raise the level of debate in this country... and let that be our legacy."

A good friend of mine is currently in a brutal season of life. She shared with me that God is not at all doing what she thinks God should be doing. Toward the end of our conversation, she spoke candidly about the current tone of her prayer life, saying, "It's a lot of yelling right now. But that's still prayer, right?" Yes, I think it is. It's the kind of prayer that takes chutzpah.

Take One For The Team

"If a man can't be cured of churchgoing, the next best thing is to send him all over the neighborhood looking for the church that 'suits' him until he becomes a taster or connoisseur of churches..." *-C.S. Lewis, Screwtape Letters*

Roughly a decade after making a public profession of faith, novelist Anne Rice publicly disassociated herself from "the Church." In her own words, she had found Christians to be "quarrelsome, hostile, disputatious and deservedly infamous..." I found her analysis of the Family partially accurate but felt her response was lacking imagination and, more importantly, grace.

Letter To A Superior Sister

You have written that your disgust with Christians has led you to believe that you "simply cannot belong" to us. I've had similar thoughts and even expressed them publicly. I understand the desire or even the need to stand some distance from the label of Christianity. But I take issue with the suggestion that you have to disassociate yourself from Christian people. Admittedly, we're a motley crew and belonging to this family can sometimes feel like being adopted by a few thousand drunk uncles. But you also wrote that you're making this move "in the name of Christ" and I think that presents a somewhat perplexing dilemma. You see, Christ hasn't quit on us and if you choose to align yourself with Him, then neither should you. Aligning myself with Christ means aligning myself with Someone who not only declared His love for all of God's children, but suffered and died in order to establish and maintain a relationship with those children. It is this redemptive sacrifice that defines His love as characteristically His. Having chosen to follow His example, it seems that at least part of the redemptive sacrifice we are challenged to make is to associate and identify with this shabby batch of miscreants who are often quite bad at following the Jesus we love. It comes at a cost but that's the nature of sacrifice. It will cost to be seen as someone related to, in your words, the "anti-gay, anti-feminist, anti-artificial birth, anti-Democrat, anti-secular humanism, anti-science" types among us. It costs Jesus to be seen as their Savior and Lord, just like it cost Him to be seen with prostitutes and the like. It is the same social role-play but seen through a different set of cultural lenses. All your statement does is swap "bigots" for "whores," when all the while they're both loved and embraced by Jesus.

It seems to me that if you set yourself against people who set themselves against people, you are likely only adding to the friction. If part of your issue with Christianity is its exclusivity, I don't think you are helping by only including those who "get it" the way you do. True Christian inclusivity means embracing both the homosexual and the gay-basher. It means working for the release of the oppressed while praying and working for the redemption of their oppressor. It means loving the beautiful game of baseball and yet, somehow, also loving the Yankees.* It means loving the Lord with all of your heart and soul and mind and also loving those who grossly misrepresent Him.

---

* *Go A's*

You have roughly labeled and dismissed people Jesus has drawn to Himself and suffered to love. Lucky for you, lucky for all of us, He is incredibly forgiving and eternally patient.

Lyrics: Take One For The Team

Take one for the team
Take it on the chin
Pick yourself back up
And brace yourself again
They don't come to fight
They only come to win
So take one for the team
And take it on the chin

Take another step
A mile beyond the call
Bear the weight of choice
To choose something at all
At times you'll want to stop
And times you'll want to crawl
But take another step
A mile beyond the call

Honestly, you should know
You've been there
Sad and low
Patience waited on you, though

So, honestly, you should know

Take a moment now
To ponder your next move
Is what you're giving back
The honest best of you
I truly understand
You've got to know I do
You took one on the chin
But you were swinging, too.

Reflection: This Is My Body, Broken

A few years ago, I attended a church service that was not at all my cup of tea. I didn't enjoy the musical style and thought the band's poor song choice was matched by how poorly they played the songs (one instance in which a double negative is not a positive). I didn't connect with the topic their pastor chose and felt somewhat alienated by some of his conclusions. It was a very traditional service and, as someone who didn't grow up going to church, I had grown accustomed to saying that I didn't have a tradition. Of course, saying that is like being the guy who tells a young lady "I'm not very good at pickup lines and so I don't really have one." If she's wise, she knows *that was* his pickup line. When it came to traditions, "not fitting in" was mine.

As I silently enumerated the ways I didn't belong in that church service, I missed the invitation to approach the front and take communion. My row had emptied into the aisle and the band had kicked back in. I cringed at the song selection again but even more at the sound of the electric drum kit. It was as if the drummer was playing a set of old Tupperware while intermittently firing off laser blasts from a 1970's sci-fi film. Moving to the aisle, I joined the others in my row and tried focusing on anything other than the music. The woman in line before me was wearing perfume I can only assume is named "Wild Berry Menthol Mist." She was wearing so much of it so that I could almost taste it when I breathed in through my mouth. Of course, the scent did take my mind off the music. Between the overwhelming scent and the sounds of The Buck Rogers Symphony Orchestra in Christ, I had to work pretty hard to keep from laughing. Of course, I knew that would be rude. And that's the difference between laughing at myself and laughing at other people, isn't it? Laughing at myself makes me more human. Laughing at someone else often means I consider them less so.

With only a three more steps until I reached the front of the room where communion was being served, I thought once again about how "these people" were not at all "my people" and how I was certainly not one of theirs. And just as I settled comfortably into my "otherness," I realized how much I sounded like a character from the C.S. Lewis allegory "Screwtape Letters." The story, comprised of a series of letters between the devil and some lesser demon, is about the devil's scheme to discourage a man from his process of faith. At one point, the principle character is sitting in a church service while the tormenting demon nudges him to look over his fellow churchgoers to see their lowliness... their otherness. The devil's hope was that this man would discover that he could not possibly belong to "those people" for many of the same reasons I was mentally distancing myself from "these people." This memory was rattling around in my head as I reached the front of the aisle. The way communion was served at this church was that, once you had been served the bread and wine, you took the elements in your hands and served the person behind you, who would, in turn, take the elements from you and serve the person behind them. This meant that "La Femme Mauvais Fragrance" would be serving me the bread and wine.

"This is the body of Christ," she said "broken for you." I took it and ate. And I lost any urge to laugh. I wanted to crawl in a hole to hide from my own shame. "This is the blood of Christ," she continued, "shed for you." I took it and drank. And I noticed it was juice rather than wine. But that didn't really matter. The matter at hand was quite literally the matter in the hands of the woman in front of me.

Bread. Simple and nearly flavorless.
Juice. Cheap and sugary sweet.

These elements, this simple matter, was symbolic of the Presence of Jesus Christ in and among "these people." The King of Heaven and Earth, Lover of Humanity, Friend to the Friendless and Voice of the Voiceless, had once again gathered a tribe of his choosing rather than a people that make Him look good to those of us with "discerning social taste." Jesus had not gathered there a people he found flavorless and cheap. He never does. He had gathered a community of people He sees as precious and priceless. And He had done so at the cost of his body and blood.

I spend a good deal of my social energy trying to surround myself with a tribe of people more reflective of my tastes and preferences. Then, at the communion table, Jesus asks me to do something dramatically different: deny my expectations, my tastes and my preferences and then receive into my life and family anyone God gives me to.

Walking back to my seat, I stood a bit closer to the middle-aged man who had been singing next to me all morning. This brother couldn't stay in the same singing key for more than a phrase or two. But how much better it is to sing off-key with a full heart than to sing with precision and not mean a word. Together, he and I sang along with the band...

Just as I am, though tossed about
With many a conflict, many a doubt,
Fightings and fears within, without,
O Lamb of God, I come, I come.

Just as I am, poor, wretched, blind;
Sight, riches, healing of the mind,
Yea, all I need in Thee to find,
O Lamb of God, I come, I come.
Just as I am, Thou wilt receive,

Wilt welcome, pardon, cleanse, relieve;
Because Thy promise I believe,
O Lamb of God, I come, I come.

-"Just As I Am" by Charlotte Elliot

Reticent

"Some things are good and some things are right
But the kids are all standing with their arms folded tight
I know it's heavy. I know it's not light
But how you gonna lift it with your arms folded tight?"
-Arcade Fire, Lyrics to "Month of May"

"People Make Problem. Droid Better."
-Ivan Vanko, Iron Man 2

This young brother initially found religion to be a kind of escape from the mess of people. But the more he encountered God, the more he found God leading him back into that mess.

Letter To A Young Brother

You have been gifted with clear vision and a critical eye. Your analyses are generally accurate. Unfortunately, you often focus of parts of the world that are dark or broken and you end up disappointed in what you see. I think your disappointment is rooted in a desire to see wholeness in yourself and in your world. Learning to trace those roots is a key part of your process.

You have often sought solitude in order to see and commune with the "Something Else" your disappointment pointed to. For a time you were convinced that whatever the "Something Else" was, it was otherworldly and that in order to get in touch with it, you had to remove yourself from the world — away from the emotional and physical mess of life together with others. But on your journey in the desert, you ran into other men. And in these men you saw something deeply reflective of the "Something Else" you were looking for. Specifically, you ran into men like Thomas Merton, who in seeking a clearer vision of God, came to the realization that such a vision would lead him right back into the emotional and physical mess of life-with-others.

In New Seeds of Contemplation, Thomas Merton wrote,
*"I must look for my identity not only in God but in other men.
I will never be able to find myself if I isolate myself from the
rest of mankind as if I were a different kind of being."*

For Merton, the goodness of God was not found only in
solitude and away from people. It was also found in and
among people. When he couldn't see goodness in people it
wasn't so much a matter of their shortcomings as it was a
matter of his shortsightedness. Merton's retreats helped him
to see God more clearly. But that clearer vision inspired him
to see God's creation more lovingly as well. For you, just as
for him, the question isn't "Is there good in the world?" In
fact, the question isn't about the nature of the world at all.
It's about the posture of your heart in relationship to the
world. The question is "can you love?"

Can you choose to be patient with people who don't get it?
Can you choose to be present to people who disappoint
you? Can you sit still over time with the messy people God
has given you in the same way you have learned to sit still in
silence and alone? Can you love? This sounds very much to
me like the kind of question God asks. I think you will find
that answering that question is powerfully confounding.
First because the answer is not static — it is not a simple
"yes" or "no." Instead, it is an answer you live out in the
process of life together with others. To answer the question

"can you love?" will mean a lifetime of choices to listen, engage, guide, help and stay. And that brings me to another aspect of this process I think you will find confounding: all the ways you can sufficiently answer the question "can I love?" will require being a physical and emotional person. The friends who know you love them are people to whom you have been physically and emotionally present — people with whom you have shared meals and conversations.

God's clearest and most powerful expression of love was similar. May it be your guide-post:

"The word became flesh and lived among us." -John 1:14 NRSV

And if it is God who has begun this work in you, as I believe it is, it means that your discontent is just the beginning of a wonderful, redemptive work.

May you hear God calling you to see that what He has made is good. May you learn to see Him where He is rather than where you think He ought to be. May you confidently know that the work God has begun in you will be finished because God finishes the works He starts. And when you are finished with the life you have been given, may you say that you saw God in the people who bear His Image that you loved Him by loving them.

Lyrics: Reticent

I hold these truths to be so good
That they cannot be understood
Were I to hold them in my grasp
Then surely they'd no longer last

I'm reticent to sign my name
To something that won't last beyond the day
I'm holding out for something real
Something I can't feel

I feel so close to everything
It's all lit up here on the screen
(I've found) What's best in life is cannot be seen
Will never be. Has never been

I'm reticent to sign my name
To something that won't last beyond the day
I'm holding out for something real
Something I can't feel

This is the way I save my own soul
I stay disengaged and stay in control

So bring on the new thing

Reflection: In Sickness And In Health

The emcee at a friend's wedding reception asked the married couples to stand. "If you have been married more than five years, please remain standing. Everyone else can sit." A few sat down. He counted upwards past ten and to twelve years, which is when Amy and I sat. "Thirteen years?" he asked and more couples sat. "Fourteen years?" and so on past twenty and upward. Eventually, only one couple was standing, he with his cane and she holding his arm.

They had been married for fifty years.
They weren't standing alone for long.

The room rose and applauded. For almost three minutes we stood and clapped while they waved and nodded thanks. I know it was almost three minutes because I was looking at my watch off and on. But I figured this couple had been married for longer than I had been alive and that was worth more applause than I normally dole out. Had that elderly couple stopped our applause and said "We've been in bliss for the entire fifty years of our marriage. It's been easy," we would almost certainly have laughed, assuming it was a joke. Any couple married more than a few months knows that couldn't be true. But it wasn't their perpetual state of happiness we were celebrating; it was their commitment to be with one another in seasons of happiness as well as in

seasons of "everything-you-do-is-annoying-right-now."
In 1998, my friend Sean Blomquist and I planted Shelter
Covenant Church. We are still pastors of that faith
community since the merciful folks there have yet to kick us
out. In the beginning, Sean and I had several motivations
for starting a church, most of which were good. Of course,
I'm not sure I have ever had completely pure motives for
doing anything in my life. It can be paralyzing if I wait until
I'm entirely right-minded before acting. Part of seeing my
life as a process has meant trusting that, as long as I'm
conscious of my mixed motives, I can move ahead into good
works and know that I will be changed as I do them. Mixed
in with our good motives for starting a church were a few
that needed weeding out. One of which was the motivation
to "do better" than what we'd seen in other churches.
Church was often such a mess: in-fighting, politics,
squabbles over carpet color etc. It looked like a bunch of
people being people and we were fairly certain we could
improve on that. In thinking this, we had unknowingly
adopted the odd, but widely held assumption that we could
improve on the "human element" of religion. We had
separated the Idea of Church from the people who brought
that idea down to earth. The problem we had with churches
was that they were made up of people who were making a
terrible racket and keeping the real business of church
(whatever that was) from happening. But when we started
our own church, people showed up who acted a whole lot

like the people we'd encountered in other churches. Furthermore, we realized that we acted a lot like those same folks, too. We looked like a bunch of people being people and were fairly confused.

Fast-forward fourteen years. As we continue to gather with people who want to follow Jesus, we recognize and even celebrate the truth that there is no escaping the human element of religion. As it turns out, religion is people. Church is people in the process of life, together. To expect otherwise is to miss the essence and beauty of religion and particularly Church.

Allow me to provide a highly unlikely scenario to further my point: Suppose my entire religious practice consisted of silent meditation, alone in a room of an empty building in an abandoned city whose citizens had been eaten by zombies who then, themselves died from side effects of the energy drink in the blood-streams of the nervous-and-shaky-but-very-alert people they had recently eaten. Even in that very ridiculous scenario, my religious practice would be learned from someone else. I may have learned it face to face or by instructional video, but I would have learned to do it by watching or listening to another person. Passing on religious or spiritual practice is always a human process. So while I am often disappointed at how messy the human practice of religion is, I am learning that removing the "human element" from the process wouldn't so much purify religion as leave us with no religion at all, which I know would make some people pretty happy... until the zombies showed up.

What I find more inspiring than my example is the story of God's relationship with people as it has been passed down by my tradition. We believe that God is not only real but knowable. We believe God revealed Himself over many years and has never shied from the "human element" of things. From the writing and assembly of the Scriptures to the lives of the prophets, priests, teachers, guides, rulers and women and men those Scriptures speak of, the whole process is riddled with limited, faulted people. I know there was a donkey involved at one point, too... there are exceptions. We also believe the pinnacle of this long process and God's fullest expression of Himself is becoming human and living with the same set of limitations you and I are familiar with; hunger, thirst, weariness, soaring gas prices, bandwidth restrictions, the abandonment and betrayal of friends etc. So, while the Church might be a ripe mess at times, we are apparently the mess God wants, or at least part of it. He has chosen us in our current state, regardless of our condition and continues to do so.

What Sean and I failed to see in our initial, critical analysis of Church was the incredible, persistent miracle of people being committed to the process of life together for the long haul. Some of the communities we had considered so messy had some serious (and some not so serious) battles raging within them. But some of the people in those communities had been fighting those battles and living life together for decades. And I think that is miraculous. I think it takes something miraculous to hold people together through thick and thin. In our better moments, Shelter Covenant Church is a family of people who have signed up to live life together for the long haul and are willing to confess that it is God who holds us together.

And that's when a church looks most like Church to me. Not when the building is clean and the coffee is hot and the walls and the chairs are comfortable. Not when the band is polished and the preacher inspires and the people stand to raise their hands in worship. Not even when we are generous and socially engaged. Those things are beautiful, true and good. But church looks most like Church to me when, after fifteen years, after twenty years or after fifty years, people stand together and say...

"I am with you.
For better, for worse,
For richer, for poorer,
In sickness and in health,
Until deaths do us part. I am with you.

When you fell apart, I stayed.
When I fell apart, you stayed.
When you couldn't pay your rent, I did.
When I broke down, you drove out and found me.
When I no longer believed, you believed for me.
When you forgot who you were, I reminded you.
When I thought too highly of myself, you helped me laugh at
myself. When you and I did not have the strength on our own
and could not find enough strength between us, we reminded
one another that Jesus holds all things together and that we
are included in "all things."

Sean and I have learned to see The Church, and our community specifically, as far more than an instrument of social and personal change, though it is that as well. The people who make up Shelter Covenant Church are a beautiful statement before we accomplish anything. We are a people bound together by common purpose and by common need. But more essentially, we are bound together by the love of God, who "has regarded my helpless estate and has shed His own blood for my soul"* and whose most consistent encouragement to His people has always been "I am with you."

---

* *From "It Is Well With My Soul" by Horatio Spafford*

Ain't No Lying Man

"Let us pause in life's pleasures

And count its many tears

While we all sup sorrow with the poor."

- Stephen Foster, Lyrics to "Hard Times"

Reflection: A Humble And Enduring Hope

A friend of mine has a teenaged son who is fighting
Leukemia. It is a terrible struggle I wish no kid had to fight.
Another young friend is living with Cystic Fibrosis. Her
treatments have become a regular part of her schedule but
they nonetheless complicate her days. Like anyone else living
with CF, her life expectancy is roughly 37 years. I know
Leukemia and Cystic Fibrosis are simply facts of life but I
don't want them to be.

On January 12, 2010, the morning after an earthquake
leveled Port Au Prince, Haiti, eventually causing the deaths
of 250,000 people, cable news networks reported large
crowds of Haitians parading through the streets between the
ruins of buildings, singing. I remember CNN reporter Wolf
Blitzer interpreting the scene as a display of "resilience and a
determined will to go on." But the songs they sang that day
(and into the night) were not all songs of resolve; they were
songs of lament, prayer and hopeful expectation. "God have
mercy," they sang as they marched. "Lord have mercy."

As they walked past mounds of concrete and rebar where
buildings once stood, they sang songs to God, the Creator.
If you are like me, you find that scene both confounding and
inspiring: A people beaten down by Creation appealing to
the Creator. And yet, where else should Haitians take their
complaint? To the Nations? Which Nation? Haitians have a

long history of being enslaved, trampled, used and abused by the Spanish, the French, the United States and others. After being treated unjustly by both humanity and the natural world, where do a people take their appeal?

I believe the desire for justice and peace is as natural and common as the desire for food and shelter, even when my desire is set at odds with the natural order of things. Among the poor, the desire for justice is perhaps more poignant because they have intimately experienced the insufficiency of Nature and humanity to satisfy it. Haitians have been decimated by economic progress, caught up in political chess playing, manipulated by get-rich religious schemes and even beaten down by natural elements. Yet many of them continue to hope in a God whose world and people have been painfully cruel. And while I sympathize with friends who see such religious devotion as somewhat absurd, I also see the absurdity of wanting reality to be different as a hallmark of the human experience — it is an absurdity most of us share in. And this is where I find religious thinking to be incredibly appropriate.

The way I understand it, religious thinking doesn't mean lazily settling for magical explanations when there are better, more reasonable and factual explanations. Sometimes dissatisfaction with the facts themselves leads me to a thought like "I know the facts but I wish it were not so."

Now, I know I share those thoughts with friends who do not consider themselves religious, so maybe calling them "religious thoughts" isn't helpful. It's simply human to wish for, long for, and even be driven by visions of a world without disease, hunger, corruption or natural disaster — a world in which people are not bought and sold by other people. And if it is simply human to desire justice, then maybe it is not so absurd to believe that desire can be satisfied. Maybe what is absurd is to possess such a natural desire for something (in this case peace and justice) when my desire cannot reasonably be satisfied.

I have come to believe these unfulfilled (and perhaps unreasonable) dreams in people are clues that there is more to life than can be weighed and measured. Just as my body's physical desire for food can be satisfied, I believe my hunger for justice can as well. When those Haitian women and men took to their broken streets singing songs of prayer and hopeful expectation, they were a living picture of what is best in humanity— the part of us that does not settle for what is simply because it is; the part that struggles, works, prays and hopes for a better world than the one we live in. I believe their persistent, relentless faith is a clue that we are made of more than matter and therefore rightly long for more than the material world can offer. I believe there is something in our nature pointing beyond Nature — something that tends toward faith. I think it is this kind of faith that drives women and men to persistently and relentless pursue cures for cancer, HIV, Cystic Fibrosis and Leukemia — faith that there is a better world to be hoped for and worked toward.

If the earthquake in Haiti on January 12, 2010 is evidence, as some suggest it is, that there is no God, and nothing beyond the observable, material world, then I find our predicament truly and terribly absurd. Nothing in Nature leads me to believe I will find hope there. Nature is characteristically violent and proceeds by the survival of whatever systems or beasts are stronger and wilier. And I certainly don't find a reasonable hope in the hands of Humanity; hands in which almost every good tool is utilized, in its turn, for some destructive purpose or held just out of reach from so many who need it unless they can pay enough for it. But I don't believe the story ends there. Instead, I join my sisters and brothers who, in the shadow of a long night when the unkind nature of Nature was displayed, took to the street to voice the humble and enduring hope God is greater in Power than Nature and greater in mercy than humanity. I join them in singing and praying as if a promise was made that we expect can and will be fulfilled.

Lyrics: Ain't No Lying Man

My God ain't no lying man
No He ain't no lying man
O Jesus, Lord have mercy
He ain't no lying man

He do just what He says
Yes, He do just what He says
O Jesus, Lord have mercy
He do just what He says

He promised me a home
Yes, He promised me a home
O Jesus. Lord have mercy
He promised me a home

And I know He will provide
Yes, I know He will provide
O, Jesus. Lord have mercy
I know He will provide

Lyrics by Dock Reed, early 1900's

Must Be Hell On You

"It's like forgetting the words to your favorite song.
You can't believe it. You were always singing along.
It was so easy and the words so sweet. You can't remember.
You try to feel the beat." *-Regina Spektor, Lyrics to "Eet"*

There are some friendships I can't imagine my life without. Most of those friendships are highlighted by a shared faith in Jesus. For a time, my friendship with this brother was no exception. As he has grown further from (and less convinced of) our previously shared faith, the friendship between us has changed considerably. But we are convinced the faith gap between us will not be our friendship's end.

Letter To A Lost Friend

I miss you in my life. I think you know that but you have never heard me say it. I miss the specific place you held in my life for many years. I remember talking with you on the phone after reading the embarrassing letters Christians had written to Richard Dawkins. You told me I was one of the few friends who helped you feel normal as a person of faith. I said you played the same role in my life. That already-short list is much, much shorter without you on it.

Your dramatic life change was, for years, the clearest evidence of God I knew. My own gnawing doubts about God were often assuaged when I remembered what God had done in and through your life. I understand now what kind of pressure that placed on you at the time. That was not my intent. I also understand now what an impact it has had on me that you no longer attribute your dramatic life-change to Jesus. Only now, after so much time has passed and we have grown more distant do I see what I lost when you, for lack of a better term, "lost your faith."

I've never blamed you for walking away. Actually, I've never thought what happened was something as simple as you "walking away." I know it wasn't just a matter of intellectual pride or your inability to deal with tragedy. To be honest, it would have been easier for me (and maybe even for you) if *something* had happened and we could sit down to work through it together. But there was nothing. In fact, that's exactly it, isn't it? At some point you found there to be Nothing where you once believed there was Something and you realized you no longer believed in God. I have never really known what to think or do about that. I wish I did. I also wish I didn't feel like I lost you. But I do.

Even from a distance, watching your process has posed a serious challenge to my own. When we were more regularly living life together you had a front-row seat to my process; you saw the inner-workings of my life and my faith. Yet, you eventually came to the conclusion that the very things I consider foundational are not foundations you can trust. Furthermore you don't even believe those things to be real. Again, I didn't have a category in which to file that. But as awkward as all this was, it wasn't the most awkward or difficult part. What was hardest for me was no longer having a convenient category in which to file our friendship. I couldn't quite bring myself to think of you as some kind of evangelistic mission target; someone to "get saved." Yet, the thing I held most dear and common between us as friends was no longer shared. I became uneasy around you and didn't know what to say. This sincerely embarrasses me. It means I had allowed the space between us to define our friendship; you were the friend I had lost. Tragically, I attributed that space to my faith and to your lack of it. But I understand now that wasn't the case. Our commonalities were never what really bound us together as friends, even when one of those commonalities was a deeply rooted and shared faith. What had always bound us together was the conscious choice we made to be friends regardless of our differences and commonalities.

What I am slowly getting to is that, while I don't entirely empathize with you (you know I've had my fair share of faith crises), I want you to know I have some sense of what you have lost as well. When your faith crisis ceased to be a crisis and became a verdict, you lost God — at least what you thought was God for so many years. You also lost several friendships whose defining characteristic was supposed to be unconditional. For a time, mine was one of those friendships. I don't want to be on that list anymore. I miss you in my life, friend. Just as you are.

Lyrics: Must Be Hell On You

It used to be, my love
The desire just to please you
Was enough to satisfy
It used to be, my love
That wanting you was easy
And your absence was a lie

So if I lose my faith do I lose you, too?
Cuz, Lord, if that's the case
Then it must be hell on you

And so it is, my love
Patience, like a jacket, can wear too thin in time
So it is, my love
Waiting in the silence wore patches in my mind

So if I lose my faith do I lose you, too?
Cuz, Lord, if that's the case
Then it must be hell on you.

Reflection: Uncertain About Faith

In March 1998 I travelled to Tacoma, WA to ask my wife if she would marry me. Of course, she was not my wife at the time, which is what made the trip necessary. At the time she was Amy Katheryn Evans, the Art Major and Young Life leader I'd met through my roommate and subsequently fallen for. I didn't bring much on the trip, a change of clothes, a sleeping bag, deodorant, an engagement ring and a toothbrush. You know... the basics. Having an engagement ring in my pocket wasn't the only thing that made this visit to Tacoma different than any of my previous visits. This was also the first time I'd shown up without telling her I was coming.

Operation "Sneaky Surprise Marriage Proposal" was simple: I asked my friend Elliot to pick me up at SeaTac* airport and then drop me off at a walking bridge where Amy and I first used the words "I" and "love" and "you" together in a sentence. The next part of my plan involved waiting on the bridge while Elliot delivered a mix-tape to Amy (yes, I made mix-tapes). The tape featured Frank Sinatra's "Strangers In The Night" and ended with my voice telling her that I was on "the bridge." I was banking a lot on Elliot convincing

---

* * "SeaTac" is an airport named after both Seattle and Tacoma. In my mind this is paramount to mixing tea with lemonade and calling it "TeaMonade" instead of an "Arnold Palmer."

Amy to actually listen to the tape and even more on Amy
listening all the way to the end.

I waited for a long while on that bridge.
I paced.
I sat down.
I paced again.
I did a set of pushups.

I don't know how long I sat, paced and push-upped on the
bridge but I know it felt much longer than it actually was.
When I get nervous, time seems to slow down (I also do
pushups). Time was moving exceedingly slow that night and
my arms were getting tired. Mercifully, it wasn't raining.
The Pacific Northwest is famous for seeing over four
hundred days of rain, annually.

Amy and I had been happily dating for quite a while and had
talked about marriage on several occasions. But now that the
moment had come for me to actually ask her "the question"
I did not know she would say "yes." I hoped she would. I
thought she would. But I was not certain. Asking her to
marry me was an act of faith; so was getting on the plane or
buying the ring. Faith has often been like that for me; having
just enough to go on but never really enough to say that I
'know' with certainty what will happen when I take a step.
If you've had conversations about the nature of faith, you've

likely heard the tightrope analogy. I'm pretty fond of it, actually. As the analogy goes, a tightrope walker stretches her rope between two buildings (and has done so tightly, one would have to assume) while a crowd gathers on the street below. With the crowd watching anxiously, the tightrope walker steps off the ledge and easily moves along the rope from one rooftop to the other. The crowd below cheers. The tightrope walker then shouts down to the crowd, asking, "Do you believe I can do it again?" To which the growing crowd enthusiastically responds, "Yes!" She, of course, makes her way back across the rope having now crossed between the buildings, without a net, twice. The crowd, now much larger, cheers again. The tightrope walker shouts to the crowd a third second time, asking "Do you believe I can cross the rope between these buildings pushing a wheelbarrow with one of you in it?" The crowd cheers in response, "Yes! We believe you can." But when the tightrope walker asks for a volunteer, nobody moves.

Two things strike me about the analogy. First, it is exactly what happened when I tried this myself. You can imagine my frustration at having purchased that stupid wheelbarrow. Not only did I keep asking for a "wheel barrel" and have to be corrected by the guy at Home Depot, I live in a condominium and have no use for a wheelbarrow. Furthermore, the analogy strikes me because it is strikingly similar to my experience of faith. So long as someone is else taking the steps, faith is an inspiring idea. But as soon as I'm being asked to "get in the wheelbarrow" I'm incredibly uncomfortable and very unsure.

I want to... and I don't want to.
I think I should... and I think I shouldn't.
I think I can... and I think I can't. Because of this, I used to think faith put me at odds with myself because it meant saying I believed things I could not empirically prove to be true:

That God exists. That God is personal.
That God is knowable.
That God wants good for me.
That God wants to be known and to know me.
That God has spoken and continues to speak and that I can hear when He does.

But I have come to believe I can say all those things and still lack faith. This is because faith doesn't mean simply saying something is true; it means acting like the things I say are true even and especially when I cannot be certain that they are true. Faith means getting in the wheelbarrow instead of watching and cheering. And in the spring of 1998, it meant getting on that plane and waiting on that bridge (and, of course, buying that ring). And so it turns out I'm acting in uncertainty all the time. It turns out that faith keeps me moving when the pursuit of certainty would almost certainly paralyze me.

Can I be certain the medication I'm taking will help me? No. But I take it, trusting what I have come to know about medicine and my doctor.

Can I be certain my job will pay enough to cover whatever expenses might come up in my future? No. But I can take that job and show up regularly to do it.

Can I be certain the words I've shared in confidence will remain a secret between a friend and I? No. But I can choose to believe his word that he will keep it.

Can I be certain that, if I trust-fall backwards off this desk, my workmates will catch me? No. But if I do hit the ground, someone will likely have caught that on video and it will a make great YouTube moment.

Can I be certain my wife and I will have a healthy child or that I'll be around long enough to raise that child?

Can I be certain my spouse is faithful and will remain so? No, I can't. I can only take her word for it and believe her character is true. And I may be wrong (as many friends of mine have painfully come to know). In fact, I could be wrong about any of these things. But if I wait to be certain before I move, chances are I will never move at all. Every major decision I have to make takes a serious measure of faith. It is faith that keeps me moving because nothing is certain.

Nothing.
Everything is seasoned with faith.

I am realizing that many of the moments I had formerly identified as "faith crises" were not moments in which my faith was being challenged, per se. They have been moments when I became more acutely aware of the challenge faith actually poses; the challenge to live without certainty and recognize the extreme limitations of my knowledge or control. My personal faith crises have never simply been moments when the dark world of doubt annoyingly calls into question the evidence I have for unseen things. They have been moments when the ease with which I've believed those things is shaken and I'm asked if I'd like to keep moving or stop. Do I still believe that what I have seen and heard was God? And in light of my uncertainty, do I want to continue living like it was?

I deeply empathize with those friends of mine who have found it impossible or at least disagreeable to have faith in God. The nature of faith as I've come to live it is dramatically different from the kind of faith my religious culture sometimes sells; a faith suspiciously similar to certainty. But I don't get in the tightrope walker's wheelbarrow because I am certain of her skill. Nor do I get in the wheelbarrow because I am certain the rope's strength. I get in because I saw the tightrope walker cross between those buildings and I think she could carry me. Internally, such a choice can feel more like a bet or even a guess, but it moves my feet nonetheless and *that's* when an action becomes faith.

I bought the ring and I got a flight to SeaTac and waited on that bridge and at no point in the process was anything certain. I saw what I thought I saw in my relationship with Amy. I heard what I thought I heard in her letters and on the phone. I thought it meant she loved me and that she would say "yes" when I asked her to marry me. She did. She's my wife now and she says she loves me and I believe her... in faith.

PART TWO: M

Heaven Knows

"We walk a while, we sit and rest
We lay it on the altar. I won't pretend to know what's next
But what I have I've offered."
-Sara Groves, Lyrics to "The Long Defeat"

"Let go of what you know
And honor what exists.
Son, that's what bearing witness is."
-David Bazan, Lyrics to "Bearing Witness"

This brother and I share a love for philosophical conversation. But we both know we can't live in our heads. I get to help him in a process I'm very familiar with myself — embodying the things I know and living what I believe.

Letter To A Stuck Brother

You deeply desire to know and speak the Truth. Your feet continually search for firm ground. You would rather say nothing than echo the speculations of the overconfident, arrogant religion of your past. I value these things about you and believe they are evidence of a Divine work in you. I know that part of what has made this work difficult is the long season of feeling restless about the Truth. Your restlessness has often led to an emotional paralysis and you have been unable to act on the truth you know with confidence. I think the season of restlessness and immobility is coming to an end and giving way to a more fruitful season. In this next season you will act on and speak of the Truth you do know with something better than confidence; courage.

You have been part of great dialogues and read many insightful texts in your pursuit of Truth. Those books and conversations have energized you and provided a sense of meaning in your process. But after all the reading and listening you've done, you have become full of other people's words. And the dissonant symphony of other people's voices swirling inside of you has left little room for your own words, and even less room for God's. As a result, the words you have often spoken have been arrangements of things you heard from parents, your past, or your former religion.

But more recently, the words of others have fallen short of your heart. You are not energized by the conversations that once energized you. You are not moved by the same ideas that once moved you. I believe this is because it is time for you to speak rather than be spoken to. I believe the season has begun in which you act on (and speak of) what you do know of the Truth rather than waiting for the next revelation or some deeper insight. Do not be afraid that you are being asked to definitively name anything, as if you have figured everything out. The time for conclusions and "naming" has passed for now and another season like it will come again. For now, your challenge is to bear witness to what you have seen and let everything else be everything else.

This moment in your process is similar to what Phillip faced when the Spirit of the Lord asked him to "Go south." There was no further explanation. Phillip just heard "Go south" and had to act on what he had heard. You have your own instruction to "Go south" and it is just as confounding in its lack of detail. But this is the heart of your "Go south" crisis — it's not about knowing what's next, it's about trusting the One who does. I believe that the next instruction you hear will only come after you've observed and acted on the first instruction.

Let whatever comes next come next.
For now, you have to go south.

Go south knowing that you know everything you need to know.

Go south knowing that your community goes with you.

Go south knowing that we have seen and heard what you have seen and heard.

Go south knowing that we believe God has spoken to you.

Go south knowing that you have never lacked for anything you are afraid of losing. Ever. God has always cared for you. He has always sustained you. You know that. But this moment is not about knowledge; it is about trust. Go south.

Lyrics: Heaven Knows

You have asked me to feed them
With my blood and my bones
But my body is burdened with concerns of my own

Heaven knows that I want to

I want to but I just can't

You have asked me to follow
To believe and obey
But the very thought of it is what keeps me away

Heaven knows that I want to
I want to but I just can't

"Do you want to get well?"
It always seemed like the strangest thing to ask a man

Reflection: Go North

I have heard it takes roughly thirteen hours to drive from the San Francisco Bay Area to Tacoma, Washington, where my wife went to college. I happen to know that if you leave with your roommate and a borrowed NorthFace dome tent in the middle of the night, travel without an atlas or cash, it can be done in closer to thirty-two.

I came to this knowledge on an adventure with my non-biological brother, Stavros. He and I were on Young Life staff together, roomed together in a place with no running water, and have shared many of our most significant adventures and moments. The particular adventure I am about to recount was one of our own making.

I'd fallen for this girl who was studying at the University of Puget Sound. Her name was Amy (it still is). After writing letters back and forth for a few months, I really wanted to see her face-to-face, so Stavros and I planned a road trip north. Now, before you go thinking this was just about me dragging a friend along on some personal, romantic pilgrimage to see a girl, you should also know about the other motivation for our journey. Stav and I had heard rumors (from Amy and others) of a particularly delectable French toast, served at a particular Vietnamese restaurant in Tacoma. So, sure, we planned the trip so I could see a girl, but also so we could try Vietnamese French Toast (henceforth referred to as "VFT").

To say Stav and I "planned" this trip is a bit of an exaggeration. We didn't really *plan* anything. We just knew we wanted to go. We didn't have much in the way of money (did I mention we were on Young Life staff?) but we figured we could work things out as we went. We also didn't know exactly how to get there. We didn't have a map. But we figured we knew the most pertinent geographical information: Tacoma was just south of Seattle and Seattle was north of the Bay Area (it still is). So, armed with the knowledge that Tacoma, the girl, and the VFT were all located north, we hopped in my 1992 Honda Civic hatchback and set out.

Stavros drove up most of the West Coast until we came to Ft. Stevens State Park in Oregon. Ft. Stevens is 4,200 acres of beauty. It is also a peninsula from which there is no way north into Washington. The sun had set long before we got there and because we didn't exactly foresee the road ending, we decided to stay in Ft. Stevens overnight. Parking my car, we grabbed the very expensive (and very yellow) NorthFace dome tent we had borrowed from my dad's jogging buddy, John Millar, and hiked through the knee-high grass to set up camp on the beach . . . illegally.

It was perfect. And it would get better.

At 5:30 am, the sun woke us when it lit up our tent in the

brightest, happiest shade of yellow I have yet to see. Stav and I crawled out of our tent and onto the sand where we sat still for what seemed like both an eternity and not long enough. We watched and listened to the intimate and joyous conversation between sand, sun, grass, and the Pacific Ocean. We were enchanted. We were also several hours behind our non-plan and really had to get moving.

We left the beach feeling like victorious pioneers. We sang with the radio like men set free from the shackles of societal expectation. And we smelled like a couple of guys who had spent the night in a tent near the ocean, which was problematic because there was this girl up north I was hoping to impress.

Leaving the peninsula meant we had to go south in order to go north — one of the moments on a journey when going backwards is the same thing as going forward. We hit Highway 101 North not knowing how we were going to deal with our odiferous dilemma. But we figured some kind of solution would present itself. Something would work out.

As we passed through Astoria Oregon, Stav pointed at a funky little hotel about a half-mile ahead and said, "Let's just ask the folks at that hotel if we can use one of their rooms to clean up." Once in the lobby, we were greeted by a cloud of smoke with a person inside it. I stepped up to the desk and said, "Um, hi. My friend and I drove up from the Bay Area last night and camped on the beach. We kinda smell bad and I'm on my way to see this girl in Tacoma and could really use a shower."

The smoke responded, "A girl, eh?"
"Well," Stav said, "there's also this Vietnamese French Toast."

A set of keys slid across the desk followed by a voice saying, "Room fifteen." *Cough*. "First floor." *Wheez*. "Bring 'em back when you're done." *Hack*.

Stav showered while I cleaned out the car. I showered while Stav returned the key to "La Dame de Fumer" and thirty minutes later we were back on the road, headed north. We arrived in Tacoma early that evening, with enough time to tell Amy and her roommates a few stories from our trip, including the small bits I just shared. Early the next morning, the entire household ventured across town to the Vietnamese restaurant where we had a breakfast that is, to this day, one of the most deeply, powerful, spiritual experiences of my life on earth.

Our journey served to provide Stavros and I a memory that will last our entire lives despite our having set out knowing very little about how we would go about it. Or maybe it would be more accurate to count the incompleteness of our knowledge as part of what made it such a memorable trip.

We traveled 900 miles, talking and laughing our way up the coast.
We slept on the beach illegally and woke up with the sun.
The Smoke Monster gave us a hotel room to clean up in because we asked.
We ate French toast of divine origin.
I spent time with the incredible woman who would eventually become my wife.
And all we knew when we left was that Tacoma, Amy, and the VFT were somewhere north and we wanted to get there.

Maybe that's why God doesn't tell me everything, because life is better when it's not exactly the way I plan it. Maybe He really likes the way I improvise. Maybe God wants me to be as creative as I am obedient. I don't know for sure. I'm just vamping on what I do know. And part of what I know is that God doesn't withhold information because He wants me to live in fear. I think God refrains from showing me the whole story because He wants me to actively live in confidence with what I do know and courageously live into the adventure laid before me. I can so easily get hung up on what I don't know that I let fear of what might happen keep me from acting. But when I can muster enough courage to step in the direction of what I *do* know, then the unknown parts of my process start to take on better names than "unsafe" and "unsure." When I act in faith, the unknown parts of life take on names like "possibility" and "adventure." Living that way has made my whole process more enjoyable and far more life-giving. Even my best-strategized and well-executed plans have been boring when compared to the experience of diving into the unexpected.

Where Believing Ends

"We do not want merely to see beauty . . . we want
something else which can hardly be put into words — to be
united with the beauty we see, to pass into it, to receive it
into ourselves, to bathe in it, to become part of it."

-C.S. Lewis, The Abolition of Man

Within my church community is a smaller community of people with whom I naturally resonate. We refer to ourselves as an "Oikos," which is a Greek word meaning "family." We share a value for art, literature, technology and a great deal else. We also share a love for respectful and honest argument. We have found that knowing the Truth necessarily changes the way we live.

Letter To My Oikos

You define meaning in your world. The sense that there is meaning in the world is to you like the sensation in the air just before it rains — the one that let's you know it's about to rain. You feel meaning in the music you listen to, hear it in the books you read, and celebrate it in the movies or artwork you see. You believe that meaning is not only there to be discovered, but also received, interpreted and responded to. You believe meaning permeates reality rather than being read *into* our circumstances. I think it is fair to say that you expect to find meaning in everything, waiting to be discovered. This expectation in you is a gift. It is a gift to believe we live in a meaningful world — a world pregnant with significance and purpose. This is one of the ways you proclaim that we live in a created world rather than a coincidental one. By expecting to find meaning in your world you insinuate God has spoken and is still speaking. Furthermore, the work you put into interpretation suggests God can be known. The care you put into doing your interpretive work suggests that knowing God will mean living differently and being more deeply connected to the One in whose world you find meaning. I love this about you and about the way we engage the world together.

That said, you have grown deeply suspicious of the traditional places where interpretation normally takes place. Churches and schools seem committed to drawing pre-determined conclusions and offering palatable answers — as if Truth was not only a predictable thing, but also something to be possessed and used. I share your suspicions. But I also challenge you to remain devoted to your own work rather than being disappointed at the interpretations of others. It is never enough to find fault with someone else's interpretation. Do not let your heart be satisfied at finding out who is wrong. Doing our own work of seeing, hearing, and faithfully acting on what we have seen of God is a much harder and more fruitful work. And that is the work we have committed to do together.

Let's not be impressed with ourselves at having insightful interpretations. Like any gift of God's, we did not earn it and cannot boast in it.

Let's never be satisfied at finding something "interesting." After its moment passes, "interesting" becomes the worst kind of boring. It replaces the thrill of actually moving with the feeling of being moved.

Let's try to add clarity to the conversation rather than try to win arguments at the expense of our common journey.

Let's chase the meaning we find and see where it leads. Not all meaning is good. So let's discern the goodness of our interpretations by evaluating the paths where they would lead.

Let's speak with conviction about the things we believe to be true so that, should we eventually concede a point, we would know a better and truer interpretation has won. Like the runner who invests every ounce of energy into the race knows that, should she lose, her opponent is faster and stronger.

Let our judgments be few and far between. Let our first priority be to bear faithful witness to what we see of God.

Let us find the value of our interpretation in relation to a long tradition of collaboration, disagreement, and conversation. It is no coincidence that the vast majority of the works we find meaningful are collaborative efforts between those who write and those who edit and those who design. Or between those who script and those who direct and those who act. Or even between those who make clay and those who form it and those who make the stoves that fire it. I think it has become clear that a beautiful and meaningful life is lived and worked out together.

And finally this: Let us work out our interpretations in a posture of humility, knowing that it is the Truth of God we seek. We do not possess or earn the Truth. Instead, Divine Truth is revealed as a gift — it enters our hearts, minds, and bodies to inhabit us just as it inhabits the works we're engaging. We do not grasp it the way a man grasps a weapon or a tool. We bear it more like a woman bears a child — we are impregnated with Truth and meaning the way the world is pregnant with Truth and meaning. And just like a woman bearing a child, our lives are utterly reshaped by Truth from the deepest parts of our person.

May the life we live together — the works, the thoughts and the culture we give birth to — be a beautiful, meaningful reflection of our Creator among us.

Lyrics: Where Believing Ends

All rise and sing
These mysterious things
On which we all agree
That's why we sing

If all you are is all we say and nothing else
Then you're just one more sad projection of ourselves
And though that might be worth something
It isn't worth my heart

So this is where believing ends and knowing starts

Some things revealed
Some mysteries sealed
So, we make a deal
And just go on what we feel

33

"You haunt me
You come back and you make me feel alone
But you're only what breaks me
So that some day I'll be whole."
-Justin McRoberts, Lyrics to "Haunted"

*Between 1998 and 2000 I wrote a series of songs about my
father's suicide. Some of those songs were released on an album
entitled 'Father.' But until this letter (and its accompanying
song) I had never written anything directly to him. It turns out
that, years later, there were things I needed to say directly;
things I needed to hear myself say.*

Letter To My Father

You were thirty-three years old when I was born.
You were only fifty-five when you decided the cards you had
been dealt could not be played and you folded.
I think of you often.
You fool.
I wish you were here.

Years after you left, when I turned 33, I woke early on that
January 1st morning, and left my house wearing a pair of
your old running shoes and your favorite jogging shirt — the
same shirt and shoes you wore the last time we ran together.
I drove to the foot of Mt. Diablo State Park, parked at the
Mitchell Canyon trailhead, and started up the valley where
you and I most often ran. Roughly a mile up the canyon is
the place where your friends, along with Mom and I,
scattered your ashes. It was a very quiet service, if it could
even be called that. A few of us shared about how much we
loved and valued you.

I missed you deeply. Everyone did.

We still do.

You fool.

I wish you had heard it.

I ran to the end of the flat trail and proceeded up the long series of switchbacks leading out of the valley toward Deer Flat. Deer Flat was as far as you and I ever ran together. It's about four miles from the trailhead and every step of the way is uphill. You were normally worn through by the time we got there. But I did not stop at Deer Flat this time. Though my lungs burned and my legs ached, I ran deeper into the mountain and through Prospector's Gap, which is as much a rockslide as it is a trail, covered with granite boulders, some the size of softballs or cantaloupe. I thought about how many times you twisted an ankle on uneven ground and how you always kept them wrapped. My ankles held through the Prospector's Gap climb. So did my knees. So did my lungs. In fact, on the morning of my thirty-third birthday, I ran the entire seven miles and over 1,700 ft. of ascent to stand at the peak of Mt. Diablo.

You never stood at the top of the mountain, save once when you came to pick me up the first time I ran to the top. That day I had done it in an act of youthful energy. But this time, on the morning of my thirty-third birthday, I did it to say something to myself and to you: I am stronger than you were. Not only am I stronger than you were the day you died, but now I know I am stronger than you were the day I was born. I was afraid for many years that might not ever be true. You were a man of great strength during your short life. Yet despite your strength you were broken by the weight of the Market's standard of success. I have had that same yoke placed on me and had feared that I would not be strong enough to cast it off.

I am.

You fool.

I wish you could see me.

So much has changed since that New Year's morning. Things have come about I had not expected. I have a son now. His name is Asa Jonathan, and his middle name is a tribute to you. His first name means "healer." Asa's presence in my life is a daily reminder that the sickness your broken culture and fractured mother passed on to you ends with me. Many times since his birth I've been struck by the realization that you didn't see this day coming.

He is your grandson.

He will never know you.

You fool.

I wish you were here.

I don't intend for this to sound harsh and I am not writing you out of anger or pride. I'm supposed to have grace for you and I do. I always have and so did everyone in your life who ought to have mattered. That is probably the most tragic part of your foolish act: it didn't matter to you that there was an abundance of grace available. You had judged yourself and had your verdict. What you didn't count on is that, in doing so, you judged me as well. Because just as you could not measure up to your own expectations, much less the expectations of your world, neither will I. None of us do, father. But you were accepted by those of us who mattered regardless of your successes and failures; you were always received in grace. And that is the way any of us are ever received — in grace. The knowledge that I am received in grace saves me from your dark fate. Grace is my strength and it will not fail. I will pass it on to my son and it will not fail him, either. My hope is for Asa to grow in that grace and in the strength it grants him. May it be with him as it is with you and I — some day he will be stronger than his father.

Lyrics: 33

At 33 I climbed the devil's mountain in your clothes
And stood there choosing to believe
what I had come to know
And reeling from the truth that I would heretofore live in

That some good thing must always die
for some new good thing to begin

You were scattered at his feet but I was standing on his neck
So, I carried with me everything of yours that I had left
To say what broke you will not break me
I am stronger than you now
I am a father with no father but I will not let my grandson
down.

Reflection: My Father, The Mountain & Me

On the wall near my desk is a picture of my father and I, taken during the 1997 Bay to Breakers race in San Francisco. He looks healthy and fit. He was. As I recall, he took off in a sprint over the final 400m of the race and I barely caught him before the finish line. We loved jogging together. It was a key part of our relationship. Some fathers and sons bond over baseball or fishing or assembling CO_2-powered rifles they then use to shoot squirrels off of power lines (you know who you are). My dad and I shared a love for jogging, and especially as I got older and was able to keep up. More than running races on city streets, my dad and I loved jogging on the dirt and clay trails of Mt. Diablo in Clayton, California.

We spent a lot of time out there, just him and me. But we also enjoyed running and hiking with my high school history teacher, John Millar. Millar was one of the merciful teachers who didn't flunk me during the academic travesty that was my freshman year of high school. He was also my track coach and became fast friends with my dad. He often invited my dad and me to join him on early morning jogs up Mt. Diablo's Mitchell Canyon trail. I was sixteen that first time and any time before 9:00 a.m. seemed not just early but unnaturally so. Most of their morning jogs happened closer to 6:00 a.m.

Millar was intricately familiar with Diablo because he spent so much time on its ridges, valleys, and trails. He knew the seasonal patterns flowers, insects and animals. Along with dragging my dad and me up the hill, he would invite groups of his students to carefully hike Diablo's lower trails each year in mid-October to see the tarantulas crossing the fire roads. Millar would literally "oooh" and "aaah" at the globe lilies when they bloomed. He also knew where there was an entrance to a hidden mine, the discovery of which made me feel like a character from an *Indiana Jones* film. He knew where mountain cats hung out and how, should we venture off the marked trail, we could make steady progress up the mountain without running into them.

Hiking and jogging with Millar and my father, I came to know the mountain as he knew it, which also meant we came to know it by the names he used. Millar called the trails by names different than the ones on the official map. For instance, about eight hundred meters up the Mitchell Canyon trail there was a small hill Millar had named after Howard Jensen, one of his regular jogging mates. A mile further, a trail branched off to the west that Millar called "White's Canyon." He named it after a friend who once took that trail instead of following Millar up the canyon and ended up lost. On most of our jogs, we would stop to stretch in an area called "The Ball Diamond." According to Millar, the Boy Scouts had built a camp there decades ago, complete with a small baseball diamond. Over years of use, the mountain's foliage grew around the diamond. If you stood where Millar suggested home plate likely was, it really did look like a Little League baseball field. Again, none of these names appeared on the maps issued by the State of California. They were known only to John Millar and those privileged few who spent time on the mountain with him. Eventually, we began to name areas of the mountain he had not previously named. We christened some of these trails and hills with names like "Braveheart Hill" and "The Meanie Greenie" trail. We even renamed a particularly hill Millar had previously called "Black Bart's." For reasons you can likely imagine, it became known to us as "Black Barf Hill."

To this day, I still know where I am on Mt. Diablo by the names I learned from Millar. The Mountain itself was and always will be "Mt. Diablo." It is too special a place for us to rename wholesale. Similarly, Diablo's physical terrain never actually changed because of what we called it. But by renaming the mountain's navigable landscape we came to know and love it as more intimately and personally ours.

The official "map" of adulthood and fatherhood bears the same names now as it did the day I was born. It is marked with trail names like "Success" and "Security" and "Provider" and "Laborer." I recognize those trails and those names because they are the names on the official map. I also recognize them as the trails and trail names my father used. The trails named "Success" and "Security" were particularly well traveled by my father's feet. They wore on his knees and ankles, making his footing less sure. They also took a great toll on his heart and eventually broke his spirit. The corporate culture he lived in for his entire adult life gave the map with those names and suggested they were the best (if not the only) ways up the mountain. I've spent enough time on those trails to decide I will call them by different names. Some of the trails marked "Wealth" and "Safety" I've renamed "Boring" and "Unhealthy." And while I will occasionally trudge up one of those trails for a season, I'll never use it for long and certainly not as my only way — there is far too much to the journey than those trails offer or the official map implies.

On the official map, anything on either side of the wide, main trail is labeled "Failure." For my dad, this meant that when he found himself off-trail at fifty-five years old, he not only lost a sense of where he was but felt like his journey was over. When the company he built was dissolved by a larger, more powerful entity, he ended up in the unnamed, forbidden space called "Failure." And that's where he quit. The tragic reality was that, so long as he was still on the mountain and as long as he had his legs beneath him, there were ways forward from wherever he stood. I cannot tell you how deeply I wish my father would have heard the better voices of friends and loved ones calling him forward and upward.

"Keep moving, Jon!"
"I'm so sorry. I just can't. I'm in Failure."
"Failure? Who told you that?"
"It's what the map says."
"To hell with the map, Jon. Look up and keep moving. We're all just a few steps away."

None of us were calling him back to the main trail. We were calling him forward and upward through the thicket and the brush toward Life. And a funny thing happens when you leave the main trail long enough: you start seeing signs of life — evidence of others having been there before you. Sometimes you find an empty water bottle or a Cliff Bar wrapper or a lost hat or a glove. But sometimes you find the lightly worn beginnings of a trail because it wasn't just one person; it was a tribe of people who had traveled through the thicket for years. Those are trails carved not by machinery, but worn slowly by the shoes and bodies of people. They are trails you have to walk slowly enough to find; trails you have to be expecting to find in order to see. They are more interesting trails, with names like "Community" and "Simplicity" and "Presence" and "Adventure." These are the trails I plan to spend my life on.

Legend has it, Spanish soldiers named Mt. Diablo after the devil when, as they chased the Chupcan toward the mountain, the Chupcan seemed to disappear. The Spanish thought it was some kind of demonic trick. It wasn't. The Chupcan simply knew how to maneuver swiftly through the prickly manzanita thicket while the Spanish, in all their elaborate garb and armor, got caught on its branches. For the Chupcan there was life off the main road and in the wild thicket while staying on the wide, main trail quite literally meant death.

Courage To Believe

"The world is a fallen world because it has fallen away from the awareness that God is all in all . . . And even the religion of this world cannot heal or redeem it for it has accepted the reduction of God to an area called 'sacred' as opposed to the world as 'profane.' It has accepted the all-embracing secularism which attempts to steal the world away from God." *-Alexander Schmemann, For The Life of the World*

Reflection: Go To And Stay Near

I was twelve years old when I met Dave Bekowies. He would show up at Pine Hollow Junior High during lunchtime to hang out. Often enough, he chose to hang out with me and a few of my other seventh grade friends. We knew Dave wasn't a teacher at Pine Hollow and that he wasn't somebody's parent. He was just some guy in his thirties, hanging around our Junior High campus. I figured that kind of thing was illegal, but it turned out that Dave was a Young Life leader and that Young Life leaders had a pretty solid reputation with the schools in my area. That didn't mean it wasn't weird. It was. I mean, didn't this guy have friends his own age? And who has time to hang out with Junior High kids except other Junior High kids? But weird or not, Dave would show up week after week and squeeze his towering 6"1' frame into the chattering, foot-shuffling, rumor-twisting circle my friends and I would naturally form when together. Once he was in, he would pepper us with questions about our lives.

During one of those conversations, Dave discovered I was playing flag football. "Neat!" he said. "When is your next game?" I was thrown for a loop. The response I'd grown accustomed to when someone learned I was playing flag football usually sounded more like, "I'm so so sorry. Is there anything I can do?" If you're not familiar, flag football is similar to football, but it doesn't involve being hit by other players or require participants to have many of the athletic skills required to play regular football — namely the ability to actually play football. That's partly why I ended up doing theatre in high school. I figured I would be wearing tights in either scenario, so I'd be better off doing something I'm actually good at while wearing them.

When I made the eventual switch from flag football to the performing arts, Dave showed up to my performances just like he'd previously showed up at my flag football games. For over six years, he would regularly inhabit the spaces I lived in and show sincere interest in the things I took interest in. He asked questions about what I was doing and what I thought about what I was doing.

I knew Dave was into Jesus because he talked about Jesus often. But when he did it wasn't weird or pushy. It was usually in the context of some conversation we were having about my life (and as a teenager, every conversation I had was about my life). When I told him I thought greed was ruining professional sports, Dave told me about the Jubilee Year in which families in Israel would receive back whatever property they had lost or exchanged during the previous forty-nine years. I told him I thought "Jubilee" was a funny name for such a cool idea. He agreed. When I was cast in John G. Neihardt's *Black Elk Speaks*, Dave and I talked about the spiritual elements of the script and he compared

some of Black Elk's lines to things Jesus said. When I was
cast in a play about nuclear de-proliferation, we talked about
war and Dave told me what he thought Jesus meant by "turn
the other cheek." Anytime Dave talked about Jesus I got the
idea that the whole "God thing," and specifically the part
about Jesus, had something to do with the life I was already
living and the things that interested me. In retrospect, I
realize now what a powerful effect this had on my faith
process — Dave seemed to see something of God in my life
even before the idea crossed my mind.

One of my favorite stories about seeing God this way
appears in the eighth chapter of Acts. The story features a
man named Phillip, who was a member of the first-century
Church, and an unnamed eunuch from Ethiopia. Phillip was
on a journey south when he met the Ethiopian eunuch, who
was riding in a chariot. Don't ask me how Phillip knew the
man was a eunuch. The Bible doesn't say. The Bible doesn't
always provide details about things I find intriguing about a
story. This is one such instance. What I do know is that
Phillip and the Ethiopian man are very different people.
More different even than a thirty-year-old father of two and
a twelve-year-old flag football player.

The Ethiopian man, besides being Ethiopian and a eunuch,
was a member of the Ethiopian royal court, where the queen
had placed him in charge of her treasury. Phillip, on the

other hand, was Greek, didn't hold an official position of power in his government and, as far as I can tell from what I've read about him, he was not a eunuch. Judging by appearances, there was very little in common between these two men. And the huge cultural gap between them makes what happens next such a powerful moment. Phillip hears the Spirit of God say, "Go to that chariot and stay near it." What a perfect choice of words.

"Go to . . . and stay near . . . " is not the language of religious agenda, which is what so many of my friends have come to expect of me because I'm a Christian. "Go to . . . and stay near . . . " is the language of a God Who went, Who came, and Who goes to His people and stays. And He does so, not because being present is the most effective means to some greater end, but because presence *is* the end. "Go to . . . and stay near . . . " is not about getting something done — it's about being present. It's about relationship.

Phillip went to the chariot and stayed there long enough to hear that the Ethiopian was reading aloud from the Hebrew Scriptures. Specifically, he was reading from verses in the book of Isaiah that Phillip's newly formed Christian community read as describing Jesus. In other words, Phillip didn't "bring the word of God" to the Ethiopian eunuch. In fact, Phillip didn't even lead the conversation. Instead, he was led into a situation he was unfamiliar with and asked to "stay." And only when he had clearly heard and seen that God was already present and active did he enter the process by asking, "Do you understand what you are reading?" The whole exchange was about what God was already up to. It was never about what Phillip could make happen. Phillip did not begin the process of faith for the Ethiopian; he was granted the opportunity to be a part of it by adding clarity.

I want to see that way.
The way Phillip was challenged to see the Ethiopian.
The way Dave saw me.

I want to assume God is present rather than wonder if He is or feel like I need to insert Him into a situation. I want to see God in more and various places and then help friends who already live in those places to see Him there. I want to see like that instead of seeing God in one, small place (on a Sunday morning around 10:00 am, for instance) and suggesting that those who want Him should meet me (and God) there. Besides finding that idea less and less true, I'm bored by it.

One of the key aspects of my faith process, especially at the outset, was coming to believe God was already present in and around my life. Dave came to the chariot I was in and he stayed. He stayed there long enough to see and hear God in my life. He was also there long enough that when he told me what he saw, I believed him. Had my friendship with Dave been mostly him telling me what was wrong with me and how I needed to change, mine would have been a very different process. Not because it would have been a less effective model of evangelism, but because it would have been a lesser part of the larger truth — God was already near to me before I knew it. He was active and alive in the places I already lived.

Lyrics: Courage To Believe

You are in the praises of Your people
You are in the silences between
You are in the wars between the nations
You are in the wars we fight for peace

You are in the absence of a father
You are in a mother's patient love
You are in dreams of friends who wander
You are in worlds they're dreaming of

Lord give me eyes to see
Lord give me strength to lead
You give me all I need. So give me courage to believe

You are in the midst of all who gather
You are in the bread and in the wine
You are in the gifts we come to offer

You are in our sacrifice of time
You are in the neighborhoods we live in
You are in the ones we're driving by
You are for the ones we call our neighbors
And the ones who still escape our eyes.

Diseases That Have Cures

"God gives us glimpses into the enormity of His work, not to increase our capacity to do a larger work or to do more work, but to make the work before us more vital and less optional. We are compelled to do the work we can do because we cannot do all we want."

I have seen this sister's heart soften and sometimes even break under the weight of bad news; specifically news about poverty and slavery. I think she looks and acts more like Jesus because she has been willing to lament.

Letter To An Affected Sister

Your heart breaks for the brokenness of things. Unlike many us who have grown accustomed to bad news, you expect things should be better than they are. I believe this expectation in you is valuable. So is your grief when this expectation is disappointed.

Don't write it off.
Don't ignore it.
Don't give it up.
You grieve because you have hope.

Neither should you give up your softness and sensitivity — they are not symptoms of weakness and they are certainly not weaknesses themselves. Instead, they are part of the great strength in you that shares in the suffering of others. Numbness and callousness are not strengths; they are compromises and they make us less human. It is better to be affected by your world than to not feel it at all.

What seems to affect you most is feeling the shadow of God loom over the tragedies you are moved by. You believe God is Sovereign and Good. But knowing Him this way has left you torn between this knowledge and what you have seen in His world. When hunger takes a life or a child is sold for sex, you wonder why God does not act? Is she not His child? This tension doesn't arise from a fault in your theology or the weakness of your faith. Our tradition is filled with faithful women and men who struggle to hold the goodness of God in one hand and the darkness of things in the other without being torn in half. Few of these saints prescribed a cognitive, philosophical relief for this tension. Likewise, I can't offer you a path to philosophical clarity and peace. Mostly what I can tell you is that I too have held my trust in God's justice in one hand and the news of some great inequity in the other, all the while hoping to find a balance and remain whole.

I can also pass along some of the wisdom I've gained from wiser people. Namely that, even if we settle on a theory by which to explain suffering in the world, all that would have changed is that we might feel better about our worldview. Meanwhile the actual pain of the actual people who are actually suffering injustice would remain untouched. The philosophical crisis you and I share seems to point to something more substantial than philosophy.

Television news pioneer Fred Friendly is quoted as saying "The role of the newsman is to create a pain in the viewer's mind that can only be relieved by thinking." I have come to believe that the pain you and I experience when looking at the brokenness of the world cannot be relieved by thinking about it, even if our thinking is right. Instead, the only relief I've ever experienced in the shadow of violence, hunger, and tragedy — the only response I've found helpful at all has not been to contend with it intellectually, but to bear whatever degree of pain I can responsibly bear. In some ways it is a luxury of the well-off to philosophize and theorize about suffering. But hunger and slavery are not just bad ideas that can be dealt with by better thinking. They are living realities. They break bodies as well as minds. It seems sensible then, for our response to real pain to be as real as the pain itself. Ideas don't alleviate suffering. Action does.

In the Scriptures, God never gives a satisfactory philosophical answer to the problem of evil. Instead, He offers the only response I've ever found to be satisfying on any level— the sacrificial action of the Cross. Certainly, there are philosophical implications to the Cross of Christ, but they are peripheral to the *act* itself. I think the pain you experience when hearing about the brokenness of your world points well beyond a philosophical problem. I think the greater effect of your pain is that it calls you to suffer with those who suffer and to do so redemptively.

So, while I believe the philosophical or theological crisis is real and that good theology matters, I also believe your fullest theological expression is the life you lead with your whole self. Which means the real crisis we face is this: we can either suffer internally because we cannot make sense of the world and its Creator, or we can suffer in a way that brings healing and restoration. You have chosen the latter path. You have committed hours and resources to care for trafficking victims. You have worked to educate others so that they do not invest in a system of exploitation. You sponsor kids with Compassion International. You have chosen to give of yourself. You have taken the Way of the Cross.

Lyrics: Diseases That Have Cures

I wrote a letter to You, Lord
Not unlike the one You sent to me
Not to explain myself or anything I think
Just to tell You what I see

Which brings us to the place we find ourselves
Where I don't know how to begin
You won't explain Yourself to satisfy my mind
And I simply won't give in.

They say Your love is great
But maybe they should wait

Until it's their child dying of diseases that have cures

They say You're faithful like the sun
I watch it rise most every day
But if I stand here still and wait here long enough
The sun will also go away

All You'll say is...

You'll say Your love is great
With Your body broken, Your spirit faint
For Your world turned over and laid to waste
While Your people treat each other like it's some damned game

But they're all Your children aren't they?
They're all Your children anyway.
Yes, they're all Your kids dying of diseases that have cures.

PART THREE: Y

Resurrection

"The ideology of our age does not believe in real newness . . .
It does not believe in the resurrection, so it must hold to
a messiah who never dies."

-Walter Breuggemann, Prophetic Imagination

I am not the best interpreter of my own life. I need the patient words of loved ones who help me see clearly. Similarly I am fortunate to play the interpreter's role in this brother's life. He had received a very narrow understanding of the Christian tradition; one in which he would never measure up. I get to remind him that God never expected him to.

Letter To a Christian Friend

In a religious culture that generally values getting life right, you have often gotten it quite wrong. Early in your Christian training, you were given hoops to jump through and lists to memorize so that you would be prepared for the ills of this depraved and dangerous world. Regardless of your hoop jumping and memorizing, you were still unprepared for that world and were conquered by it. You "failed." And when you failed, you not only failed yourself but you failed the religious system designed to keep you from failing.

You had the horrible misfortune of losing favor early in a culture wherein favor was hard-won. The way was paved for "failure" to become a defining characteristic of your relationship with God and His people. When you floundered, you weren't so much disappointing people as you were meeting the low expectations they already had. You learned to expect of yourself the same thing: at some point you would fail. You have lived long seasons waiting for the other boot to fall and believing that, even when favor was granted, it would not last.

I do not think your early religious training provided you
with enough light to accurately evaluate your life's process.
Nor do I think you were provided an accurate definition of
"failure." Yours is not a story of a man who "can't hold it
together," though many things have fallen apart in your
hands. It is not the story of a man who constantly sabotages
his own good fortune, though you have often shot yourself
in the foot. You are not a man whose past mistakes will
haunt and corrupt the landscape of your future, even if the
past haunts you now. Your story is not a story of failure; it is
a story of boundless mercy. It is a story about getting second
chances seven times, and then seventy times that. While
some would suggest your life's process was marked by failure,
I believe that it is characterized by grace.

On one hand, the sad reading of your history is accurate.
How many times has your life nearly imploded? How many
times have you schemed your way into some corner and
found yourself stuck only to convince yourself the only
escape was yet another scheme? How many corners have you
found yourself in? Even now you find yourself in yet another
corner after another botched plan. But this time you haven't
tried to work your way out. This time, you stopped and
waited to be caught. In part you stopped because you were
exhausted from years of running. You also lost faith in your
own schemes. In the past, you thought being caught would
mean being exposed as a failure once again — meaning yet

another cycle ending in shame, judgment, and punishment. But you have not found shame or judgment or punishment this time. Being caught in this corner has meant experiencing the firm grasp of God and those to whom He's given you. That grasp has held you in place long enough to hear the voice of the Father and His family saying, "You are forgiven. You are loved. There is grace here."

Along with providing a narrow and destructive definition of what "success" in the practice of Christianity looks like, your Christian training failed to teach you that failure to achieve that goal is not a dead end — it is a doorway. And through this doorway you have found a better foundation for life than performance.

Only because you "failed" as a friend have you come to know who your true friends are. The foundation of those friendships cannot be easily uprooted.

Only because you "failed" as a son have you come to know that the true love of the Father is unmoved by your performance. This also means you can *be* a true father. Only because you failed the religious culture of your youth have you learned that God never asked you to live up to that culture's standards in the first place. Instead, with every failure, He has held you together and kept you from completely undoing yourself. At every moment in your process, God has granted you His favor. And He has done so, not because you have pleased the Father with your performance, but because you are His. And *that* is all He has asked you to be.

Resurrection

It's not about the drinking
It's all about being drunk
It's not with whom you're sleeping
It's with whom you wake up

It's not about the wars you fight
It's whether or not you win
Not so much about being right
As not letting all the wrong ones in

We all want that resurrection
But we don't want to die
We all want that sweet salvation
Without the bitterness of sacrifice

It's not about forgiveness
But making sure they know
You're the one they've injured
But you're too strong to let it show
It's not about believing
It's about making it look good

So when you loose your reason
You just keep doing what you should

The Fear Of God

"They all pose as if they had reached their real opinions through the self-development of a cold, pure, divinely unconcerned dialectic while at bottom it is an assumption... most often a desire of the heart that has been filtered and made abstract."

-Friedrich Nietzsche, Beyond Good and Evil

The critique of religion offered by my atheist friends has been a vital and necessary part of my faith process. This long-time friend holds a dear place in my heart and his challenge to my faith has at times been a refining fire. I hope my faith in Jesus can be the same for him.

Letter To An Atheist Friend

The idea that anything beyond observation is absurd to you. But for anything to be beyond moral judgment is more than just absurd to you, it's offensive and dangerous and particularly if such a quality is attributed to a person. They could ask terrible things of you and me — things we consider contrary to our understanding of what is "good." In light of this, I identify with your vexation at the casual nature with which Christians talk about the "goodness of God." Your criticism of such talk exposes the lack of sobriety with which we say such things. I agree that calling God "good" should not be a cursory remark; it is often a choice to believe something that is radically contrary to observation.

It seems it is not the general idea of religion you find distasteful but the measurable damage you see religion doing. You are convinced people would be better off without the influence of religion. Belief in God appears to open the door for all forms of violence to be permissible so long as God has sanctioned them. Furthermore, what you find in the Scriptures is not a God who assures you that He would never do something contrary to common decency. Instead, you find a God who reserves the right to flood the earth. It is this, above all else you cannot observe without making some noise about it. I think your indignation regarding religion's damage to human life is understandable and honorable. I also think it is rooted in a value for life and a love for people which you and I share.

But while you and I share this value and want to see those we love live a good life, our points of reference are markedly different. For my part, I believe the good life is rooted, quite literally, in relationship with the Creator. Not only in the often over-sentimentalized invitation to have a relationship with Jesus, but also in the basic philosophical notion of "goodness." For instance, you and I agree it is good for children to be fed, learn to read, write, grow up in health, and then pass on that good life to their children. We also agree it is wholly evil for young girls to be bought and sold for sex slavery. By saying such scenarios are "good" or "bad" suggests they meet or miss a standard of goodness we both agree on. On a much larger scale, the sweeping sentiment that human life is good and ought to be preserved also appeals to a standard beyond our preferences but to which you and I once again agree upon. I express this standard by saying the Creator wants His kids to live well and be healthy. I know you find this idea problematic. In many ways, so do I. Part of what this means for me is that when my will differs from the Creator's will, I am not only in the wrong but possibly detracting from what is good in the world. Ultimately, such a crisis of wills must be resolved in my submission to the Creator. Not because I find His will more appealing or better suited to my sensibilities, but because His will is the standard of goodness. As I've shared with you before, the crisis of wills can be strange and uncomfortable, but it is not where the fabric of my devotion begins to unravel. Instead, these crises are actually the essence of faith as I've come to know it — choosing to call "good" what God calls "good" when I do not see it that way. My value system is rooted in faith.

And this is where my challenge to you begins. I believe your value system — your vision for what is good — is as much a matter of faith as mine. I see this most clearly in the value you attribute to humanity. I don't believe you developed a value for human life after a careful examination of the facts. I think you continually choose to consider human life valuable, even in light of facts that might easily suggest otherwise. After all, if there is nothing more to reality than what we can see and measure, then a significant portion of what we see is a history of people committing horrifying acts of violence against one another. Furthermore, those acts are sometimes justified by way of an elaborate, manipulative lie people have invented called "religion." In this light, it seems you and I share a crisis of sorts. Just as you ask me why God is worth believing or following, I ask you why a species such as ours is worth valuing and preserving. And I think we both have to answer with statements of faith. In your case, you simply believe human life has value, regardless of the mountain of evidence I could cite to the contrary. Again, I see that as a choice you make. And it isn't an uncommon choice. In fact, it is remarkably similar to the choice most of us make to love other people — parents, kids, spouses — not because of any merit on their part, but because we've simply chosen to. This characteristically unreasonable choice is what I've come to see as the heart of love. And I see it in the way you value people.

Love, as I understand it, is no mere sentiment and no simple matter of chemicals mixing in your brain. It is the choice you and I make to care for and help people even, and especially, when the choice is unreasonable. Love is not established by evidence or in a reasoned evaluation of the facts. Rather, love establishes value and everything else grows from its soil. In your case, your love for people came first and your critique of religion grew out of it. I see your value for human life as a display of love rather than the end of a reasoned analysis. Perhaps it would be fair to say that love, rather than reason, is the lens through which you see people and determine our value? If you are right when you suggest there is no Creator and no universal standard of value, then it is all the more vital we live according to what we cannot see or measure or establish by evidence. Because in that case, the value of those we love could only be established in our choice to love them.

That being so, may the Truth as you see it never become more important to you than the people who know it (or don't). May your heart continue to grow fond not just of the Truth as a concept, but of the most real thing in what you believe to be a strictly material world: the people who live in it.

Lyrics: The Fear Of God

My God knows everything. He knows my mind
And that's what has me worried all the time
My God sees everything. He sees my heart
And I think that's the most disturbing part

Cuz I know some of what's inside of me
It makes the whole thing harder to believe

The fear of God. They say it is the beginning of wisdom
I'm scared as hell. So tell me when do we begin?
The fear of God. They say it is the beginning of wisdom
Am I ready yet to learn?

My God does anything He wants to do
And when He does, it makes the action true
But there are things I know my God has done
That strike me both strange and even wrong

Your thoughts are higher than... So, can I question them?

Reflection: Some Men Just Want to Watch the World Burn

I recently sat in line to catch the 3:45 a.m. debut showing of *The Dark Knight Rises*. I had missed getting tickets for the midnight showing (a failure I count among the most grievous errors of my life). Sitting in the hall at San Francisco's Metreon, I could feel the thunderous sounds of the movie shake the wall I was trying to sleep against as several hundred fortunate others watched inside. When the midnight showing ended, I rose with my haggard compatriots and readied myself for the most anticipated movie experience of my life. I noticed a group of young men who had just seen the film bounding toward me. It took me a few moments to realize that, as they drew nearer they were barking out spoilers. People in the line around me covered their ears, booed, and hissed. I had actually prepared myself for such an event and hit "play" on my iPod shuffle, sending the deep, soaring sounds of Hanz Zimmer's *Dark Knight* soundtrack into my ears.

Eventually, the kids barking spoilers left the room and the noise died down. A young girl in the line before me moaned, "Why would someone do that? Why would someone try to ruin the movie for us?" I couldn't help but think of the poignant line offered by Bruce Wayne's butler, Alfred Pennyworth, in the previous Batman film *The Dark Knight*. "Some men," Alfred said, "just want to watch the world burn."

People do terrible things to other people. Perhaps better said, we do terrible things to one another. It has become increasingly popular (and easy) to point at religion as the poison in humanity's otherwise generally healthy bloodstream, causing otherwise good people to do terrible things. Theoretical physicist* Steven Weinberg is often quoted as saying, "With or without (religion) you would have good people doing good things and evil people doing evil things. But for good people to do evil things, that takes religion." As poignant as Weinberg's critique is, I think it still misses the point, and not because it offends my tradition. It misses a unifying Truth larger than my tradition and that of critical atheism — some men just want to watch the world burn and the right-minded among us don't want it to.

The critique of religion offered by my atheist friends has been a vital and necessary part of my faith process. They dare me to face my faith claims and religious practices from views outside of my tradition. They push me to distinguish between things I wholeheartedly believe and things I only claim to believe. They perform a service few within my tradition can perform, sincerely challenging the roots of

---

*
    Calling Weinberg a "theoretical physicist" does not mean he is only a physicist in theory. He is actually a physicist. His particular field of expertise is called "theoretical physics" which means, I believe, he writes scripts for the SyFy channel.

faith without the safety net of cherishing the same faith. Usually, when a pastor offers faith-challenging questions, I can safely assume the crisis they pose will find resolution in the end — like a crisis in an adventure film. I always know Bourne or Bond or Batman will somehow make it out alive, get the girl, and win the day. But when the same critique is offered by someone who does not cherish my faith or the tradition in which I practice it, I know the blade is sharp and is capable of separating flesh from bone, fact from fiction, and true religion from the consumer garbage I have too often accepted in place of a fully flourishing, complex, and living faith.

As I hear it, the atheist critique of religion is rooted in some of the same soil as my religious thinking. First it begins with a kind of confession: there is something about ourselves we find deeply troubling, if not simply flawed — the part that inspires us to make an awful mess of otherwise good things. Secondly, the atheist critique is desirous of a reality that is not reality. My atheist friends and I share the wish that things were better than they are — we wish for more enduring peace, more equality, less illness, and the absence of damaging ideas, which includes at least certain kinds of religion. Finally, and most compelling to me, atheism's critique of religion shares the same root value as religion — that life, and particularly human life, is intrinsically valuable. In this light, I'd suggest that if I isolate my critique of human violence to violence done in the name of religion, I make too small of a statement. So, while I agree religion can serve as a potent additive to hatred, I think it is in no way the only or even the most potent additive.

—The over 200,000 Japanese citizens killed by atomic weapons in August of 1945 weren't killed for religious reasons. Those bombings were planned, executed, and justified on political grounds. So was the war the bombings were part of and the development of those weapons in the first place.

—The 800,000 Tutsi women, children, and men shot, burned, and hacked to death in July of 1994 weren't killed for religious reasons. That disgusting hatefulness was racially motivated and fueled once again by politics and economics.

—Motivation for the African salve trade was not religious. It was thoroughly economic. The driving force behind the modern day slave trade is also economic. The millions of people held in some form of slavery today — many of them children trafficked for sex and labor — are disposable pieces in a greed-driven, horrifying black market economy. Even if I accept Weinberg's evaluation of religion as an invention of humanity (like economics and politics), I'm still left with people inventing ways to do harm to one another. All I would do is add religion to the list of harmful inventions. No matter how long the list gets I am still faced with the basic fact that we do terrible things to one another. No matter how long the list gets, I still have the deep conviction that things should be other than they are. And this is where my atheist friends and I can begin to reason together. We agree something is wrong and that something seems to poison just about everything: art, economics, politics, and even religion.

In his book *Desiring the Kingdom*, James K.A. Smith suggests that everyone lives with some vision of "the Kingdom." While the expressed details of that Kingdom may be different (example: my wife really wishes there was a "Free S'mores" stand on every corner) the common desire for things to be different and better than they are is a shared human desire. This agreement paves the way for productive conversation rather than engaging in the kind of ideological competition in which I must defeat my enemy to make room for my perspective. And in conversations with atheist friends, I think I can be helpful so long as I'm not trying to win an argument. Just as I think it can take an irreligious perspective to help point out a blind spot in my religious thought, I think it often takes a religious or metaphysical perspective to point out the blind spots in atheism — namely the baseless, improvable, and utterly necessary assumption that life is valuable.

I think good religion expects God to be up to something everywhere, which means expecting God to be present and active outside my own religious tradition. I think what God is up to isn't about religion or atheism; it's about people. Some of those people call themselves "religious" and others call themselves "atheists." If I am constantly standing at the ready to defend my tradition from the attacks of those outside of it, I just may deafen myself to the voice of God "out there." I also miss the humanity of those not in my camp who, before they are anything else, are God's beloved ones. I have found most of the challenges offered by atheists are not couched in a hate-driven, maniacal desire to eradicate faith so that they can control the world from their technologically advanced lair-of-evil, hidden in the heart of a volcano and decorated with the remnants of demolished churches. I don't think that's what atheism is. I've come to see atheism as a worldview in which many friends find hope — some of them after multiple encounters with poorly developed and poorly practiced religion. Atheism is a worldview in which religion is problematic insofar as it is an obstacle in a fully flourishing human life. Sometimes it is. So while I'm not willing to embrace atheism as a completely right way of thinking, I'm also not willing to hear their criticism as the voice of my enemy bent on destroying the tradition and world I love. I want to hear them with ears that expect God to be up to something everywhere, regardless of my expectations and preferences. Relegating the activity of God to only the spaces I've designated for "religious" activity is part of the bad religion my atheist friends are right to see as an obstacle to human flourishing.

Expectation

"A life can be launched with as little as a single word."
-*Wess Stafford, President of Compassion International*

Reflection: Expectations

In a dusty, broken village outside Calcutta, a young woman named Sevita expects to become more than her culture believes she can be. Her brother, Deephalder, expects Jesus to hear him when he prays. And somewhere in Canada, teenaged girl expects to change the world by writing letters. The story God weaved between these three people has changed my expectations.

I expected my trip to India to be like other international trips I had taken. It wasn't. India was a whirlwind of color and sound and smell, darkness and light and death and life, which makes it sound a bit like Las Vegas. It isn't. Friend and travel veteran Suzie Johnson wisely suggested I take mental snapshots of key moments instead of trying to boil down my time in India to a single anecdote.

—The sun never touching the horizon in Calcutta; just changing from pale yellow to dark red and disappearing into a gray-brown soup.

—The beauty of India's women transcending the ugliness of the caste system.

—Traveling for hours by train and never coming to a place that didn't feel crowded.

—Stepping over what I thought was a pile of cloth on a crowded sidewalk, only to discover it was an infant, wrapped in rags.

I also remember every moment of my time with Deephalder and his older sister, Sevita.

Deephalder walked briskly and confidently as he showed us around the school he attended. "We eat together here," he told us. "This is also where we sit to read." He is very fortunate to go to school. Considered nearly worthless by the dominant culture, he and his family are called "Untouchables" and are generally disallowed access to medical care or formal education. But Deephalder's school is hosted by one of Compassion International's church partners. And thankfully, the folks there think differently of Deephalder than the dominant culture. So does the teenager who sponsors him. Together they believe that, far from being worthless, Deephalder is a priceless and beloved child of God, the same as you and me. And because they believe this about him, they help provide Deephalder with food, medical assistance, and education.

"Come, please. Meet my family," Deephalder asked us. The translator added, "He would like you to call him 'Deep.'"
I told him I thought he was awfully "deep" for a twelve year old. Deep did not laugh, partially because he does not speak English and partially because it was a terrible joke.

We met Deep's family in a hut no larger than my childhood bedroom. I could see the yellow-brown glow of the afternoon sky through the bamboo, sticks, and leaves making up their roof. "Does it rain a lot?" I asked . . . and then waited several minutes while the translator conferred with other people in the hut. As it turned out our translator was not familiar with the dialect Deep's family used. Several minutes later and after numerous interchanges between translators, the response came back, "The family says they do not like fish." The translation issues made the conversation difficult. But it was worth the effort.

Deep's father stepped forward and said, "You can see I am very thin." I could count the bones in his back through his shirt. "I am not thin because I do not eat. I am thin because I could not walk or use my arms for a year." I asked the translator to clarify. "Is he saying he was paralyzed?" She conferred with the other translators and a few members of the family and several minutes later turned back to me, saying, "Yes. He fell off a roof and broke his neck. Also, he says he does not like fish." Deep's father was standing firmly upright and had his hands on his son's shoulders. "I lay here for a year," he said, gesturing toward the dusty, red mat at our feet. "My family cared for me. But we had no work. Then my son started reading us the stories his sponsor sent us in her letters. She wrote about Jesus healing people. We had never heard those stories before." He looked down at his boy, who was beaming while his father spoke. "Deephalder believed those stories and asked the Christians at his church to pray for me." I will never forget the long silence in the hut after he said, "After they prayed for me I stood up."

That was not what I expected to hear.
But that is what Deep expected to happen when he and his friends prayed.

After two hours of linguistic gymnastics and soul-bending stories, we weaved our way through brick mounds and banyan trees until we were halted by a small, clear, cheerful voice saying, "Thank you for coming to our home, it was very nice to meet you." It was Deephalder's older sister Sevita, waving and smiling. And while I know my first question should have been, "Where did you learn to speak such perfect English?" It wasn't. My first question was, "WHY DIDN'T YOU HELP US BACK THERE!?"

"You did very well," she said. It would appear that standards for Americans in international conversation have fallen off a bit.

Sevita told us she taught herself English. She said her brother Deep was always inspired by his sponsor's letters. She wanted to read those letters they way they were written. So she sat for hours comparing the handwritten English letter with the Hindi translation. "Eventually," she said, "the English started to make sense." That blew my mind. She's fourteen and lives in a mud hut. I'm thirty-nine and have a Bachelors in English Lit but still confuse the proper use of "whom" and "who." My friend Steve asked Sevita what she was going to be when she grew up. She didn't hesitate before she said, "I am going to be a banking manager."

Sevita lives in shocking conditions and is considered sub-human by many in her culture. On top of that, she's growing up in an environment in which she is generally considered a second-class citizen because she is a woman.

And yet she expects to run a bank.
Why would she expect such a thing?

As it turns out, the teenager who sponsors her brother often writes about her mother. Her mother is a bank manager in Canada. Sevita expects to become more than her culture says she can for the same reason Deep expected Jesus to help his father — because her teenaged sponsor is telling better, more beautiful stories. She is telling stories that don't end in physically or emotionally paralysis; stories in which Deep and Sevita aren't untouchable.

I have come to believe that there is no default setting in the human mind. My expectations, along with a large portion of my identity, are formed in me by the words and the presence of others. I may believe I am trash or I may believe my life is of immense value, but I don't arrive at either conclusion after a sterile observation of simple facts. I believe what I believe about myself because I've been convinced those things are true by the voices I allow into my life. The expectations I have for myself and for my world are developed in relationship with others and I hold them as articles of faith. Part of what this means is learning the way my voice plays an essential role in the process of people I love. If those people don't know I love and value them, I have to let them know.

Lyrics: Expectation

Lord, You know we've seen it
Wealth without the work
And pleasure with no conscience
Both plagues upon the earth
We are overwhelmed; we are overcome
And yet we live in expectation

Lord you know we've lived it
Religion with no cost
Worship that means nothing
Because it does not bear a cross
We are overwhelmed; we are overcome
And yet we live in expectation

Science without a heart
Knowledge with no character
Politics without a sense of place
And we're selling things without a thought
For what it is we really want
And what it is they really cost to make.

Remember Me Jesus

"Most of us come to the church by a means the church does not allow." *-Flannery O'Connor*

I have seen friendships leveled by theological or political disagreements. In this light, I hold my relationship with this sister in high regard. Our differing opinions have never defined our friendship much less endangered it. In and through our differences, we have come to believe we are bound together on levels far deeper than our opinions or preferences.

Letter To A Queer Sister

We are not alike, you and I. We do not always agree. Our disagreements are often about things that can end friendships— pressing and vital issues about God and our identity. I'm deeply thankful that agreement is not the foundation of our friendship. We've come to see, despite our differences of opinion, that we share the same *core* identity: we are both Beloved. Which means our disagreements, far from being detrimental or terminal for our friendship, can instead enrich it, adding depth to both our lives and bearing fruit between us.

You have always taken the matter of your identity very seriously. Even your formal education has been more about developing a sure foundation for knowing who you are than it has been about career preparation. The discipline of academic study has provided a way to solidify, verify, and at your lesser moments, justify your identity. Your process has been a joy to watch and share.

Including your education, the path you've taken towards
identity has rarely been a straight one. It has been strewn
with obstacles sometimes set before you by history,
sometimes by dumb luck, and often enough by your own
hand. Even at this early stage, much of your process can be
fairly characterized as "queer." But there is far more to you
than being "queer." Despite the apparent chaos of your
process, you have always had an urgent desire for
community. And regardless of the oddity of your way, you
have always had a pressing sense of purpose and direction.
Whatever benefit being "the outsider" might have afforded
you in the past has been overtaken by your joy in belonging
to a particular people, in a particular place, and feeling at
home. You have longed to be folded in without being
smothered. You have dreamed of helping to shape a truly
graceful community — one characterized by the loving work
of reconciliation. While you will not (and should not)
conform in order to fit in, you are discovering that the
difference between you and others is not what is most
important about you. You are more than queer. You are
more than odd. You are more than the lovable outsider.
Before you are anything else, you are Beloved.

You did not academically determine that you are loved nor
did you develop such knowledge by way of religious practice.
You did not carefully craft your "belovedness" and did not
unearth it from layers of false identity, though there is some

value to that process as well. Instead, you have slowly, and sometimes reluctantly, *received* your New Name from the loving and patient hands of those you have allowed to access your heart. You have embraced your New Name even as you have allowed yourself to be embraced by the One who calls you "daughter" as well as by those who call you "sister." What a great mystery this is: we are not what we make ourselves. We become who we are by the love of those we allow to love us. Our identity is a gift.

Furthermore, by embracing yourself as "Beloved," you are embracing a shared identity — it is not your name alone. You share your identity with me and with a whole tribe of others — many of whom you and I would not have chosen to call "Beloved" if it were up to us. You and I will always live in community with people who, though they share our core identity, do not share our worldview or our tastes and preferences. We did not choose them. God chose them just as He chose you and me. He drew them near just as He drew you near. And so long as you and I remain near to God, we will be surrounded by sisters and brothers with whom we do not agree. Some of those people will be close friends.

Of course, You are familiar with being in such a position. For years, you have wrestled with your culture and your community over these very things. Similarly, you have wrestled internally about who you are, and have sometimes wished you did not believe what you believe about yourself or about your world. Some of those internal conflicts remain in you. But just as the conflicts between us are redemptively framed by the common identity we share in Christ, the conflicts within you are framed by the foundational reality of being fully known, fully embraced and newly named by the One in whom there is no conflict.

May you continue to know yourself as Beloved. May you learn to trust God more easily than you trust yourself. May wanderers and outsiders find you among them and know they are loved by you. May you have the courage to lead those whom you love to a place they can call Home — where they can know themselves as "Beloved."

Lyrics: Remember Me Jesus

Remember me Jesus. Remember my name
When you come to your Kingdom
Where forever you'll reign
See, I'm so forgetful, I've forgotten my way.
So remember, remember, remember my name

Have mercy, My God on this old, tired soul
I'm aware of my deeds, aware of their toll
The strong ones repent, Lord
The week ones just fold
So have mercy, my God, on this old, tired soul

Will you stay with me Jesus? Stay here all night
I am all out of anger
And I'm too tired to fight
I've heard you are faithful and patient and kind
Would you stay with me
Would you stay here all night?

Reflection: Nathan, God's Son

I made a gay friend in college.

That's something I used to say as a point of pride. I thought it made me sound dangerous and cool to my Christian friends. Eventually I realized that trying to sound cool by bragging about having a gay friend was paramount to bragging about owning a rattlesnake — it might make me sound cool and dangerous, but it also made my friend into something more of an idea than a person.

It didn't take long for me to discover Nathan was queer. Our first meeting was a strong indication. He was late to the first day of our Philosophy of Art class. With only eleven of us in the class, Nathan's entrance was very noticeable and not just because he burst through the door while the professor was giving his opening lecture. It was also because he came through the door wearing gold, leather pants and sporting leopard print hair.

Leopard.
Print.
Hair.

I took a wild guess he was gay.
It turns out I was right.

On the other hand it took me some time to figure out that Nathan was a Christian. I found out at a party thrown by the Philosophy Club. Yes, I went to Philosophy Club parties. In all honesty, those parties made up about half of my collegiate social experience . . . the grown-up half. My other social outlet consisted of spending time with gaseous, chain-smoking, sixteen-year-old skate-punks as a Young Life leader. What great mercy God granted me that I met a girl who lived out of state and never actually saw the anemic nature of my social life.

During a particularly tense conversation at the Philosophy Club party, I found myself looking down the barrel of a rather loaded critique of Christianity. St. Mary's is a Catholic college, but the majority of the folks I met in my classes were not friendly toward religion. This was definitely the case with my Philosophy Club friends, among whom faith was widely considered a weakness of thought and an intellectual compromise. A few jabs into my philosophical boxing match, Nathan came to my defense. He spoke eloquently about the philosophical foundations of his faith and pointed at the assumptive nature of our friends' critiques. He was gentle and confident and gracious. I was dumbstruck. At that point in my life, listening to a homosexual claim to believe in Jesus was like seeing a unicorn. Only this unicorn was gay and claiming to be a Christian. I didn't have a box in which to put the unicorn. Yet there he was, waxing philosophical and full of faith.

I told Nathan afterward I hadn't known he was a Christian. He said that was okay because he didn't wear it on his sleeve the way I did. Beyond joking with me about the way I carried my faith, he was referring to the tapes of my music I had given him. The songs on those tapes were rather overtly evangelical. I'd given him the music in part because I wanted to tell him about Jesus. You know, help my gay friend give his life to Christ since those two things — being gay and knowing Jesus — were diametrically opposed , . . right?

The conflict never came up in conversation between the two of us, though it was in my head whenever we hung out. What was he? A Christian homosexual? A homosexual Christian? A unicorn? My inability to fit him into the categories I normally used to control my world became one of the better gifts God has given me. Because of that gift, I ceased looking at Nathan through the filter of his sexuality. He wasn't a homosexual first and then a Christian. I also stopped seeing him through the filter of his religion. He was not a Christian first and then a homosexual. Before any of that, he was my friend, Nathan. And I've come to believe that is probably the way God sees him, too. I don't think God sees Nathan as His gay, Christian son or His Christian, gay son. Nathan is God's son. Everything else, no matter what it is, comes second. Shortly before graduation, Nathan gave me a painting of his. It was a painting of Jesus, crucified. Jesus' head is tilted toward his right shoulder and toward the perspective of the observer. His eyes are closed, though not in the way a man closes his eyes when he's in pain — more the way a man closes his eyes to sigh, in sadness. It's a striking image not only because it is a crucifixion but also because it looks to have been painted in a fit of emotion. Nathan's brush strokes feature prominently on the canvas and the paint is laid on pretty thick. The way the piece was painted challenges me to engage with the artist whose piece it is as much as with the subject of the piece. In other words, there is a lot of Nathan in his painting of Jesus. And I think there is something very appropriate about that. Looking back on the picture of Jesus I was trying to paint with music, I can see a lot of myself there as well. Thankfully, Nathan recognized Jesus in my music, which is to say that Nathan saw Jesus in me. By giving me his painting, Nathan was giving me a way to remember how I had seen and recognized Jesus in him. It was this shared vision that bound us together. Our differences, disagreements, and misunderstandings came second.

Where All the Colors of the World Collide

Every poem different but
Telling the same story
And we've been gathering
Them in a book
Since writing began
And before that as songs
Or poems people memorized
And recited aloud
When someone asked: "What is life?"
-Gregory Orr

Letter To My Son

Asa,

You are my son and I love you.

Dad

Lyrics: Where All the Colors of the World Collide

You find the reasons for the life you're living
Are predicated on what is not best
This is the good life
This is the start of things at last

When the lament over your absent father
Becomes a story that can heal a soul
This is the good life
This is the life becoming whole

When you no longer know what you can call it
And yet you move despite the fear and doubt
This is the good life
This is the life of courage now
And you find yourself singing out . . .

When grace begins to heal the wounds it caused you
And every footstep falls on holy ground
This is the good life
This is the life of here and now
So when you're finished tearing down the whole thing
And you're undone by all the good there is
This is the good life
This is the life you get to live
May you find yourself singing out . . .
Where all the colors of the world collide

Reflection: Zablon, Asa and Me

This project, the book, and its accompanying music began with a letter from a young man in Kenya. His name is Zablon. The words of his letter helped to revive an enormous part of my life's process that I thought had died. Years before I read Zablon's letter, I found and read a short letter my father had written to me.

"Son, take care of your mother.
I love you both so much.
Too much to drag you into my depression.
I'm so sorry, I just can't ... "

The note, written in pencil on stationery from his recently defunct travel firm, trails off in a few scribbles but remains unfinished.

To be clear and fair, my father was not a cold person. On the contrary, I remember him as a kind, generous, and funny man. I remember how he loved Elvis Presley. I remember how well he danced with my mother. I remember him wearing a Darth Vader mask while coaching my Little League soccer squad so we would pay attention. His good humor and warmth were part of why the words of his note had such terrible force. They rang in my soul like a well-struck musical note rings out in a concert hall until the walls are themselves ringing with it. Normally, you don't know what note a room will resonate with until the actual note is struck. The words of my father's note rang clearly and definitively in my soul, "I'm so sorry, I just can't . . . "

And then I read Zablon's letter.

Amy and I had sponsored Zablon for nearly a decade through Compassion International. We had also recently met him when some generous friends at Compassion helped us get to Kisumu, Kenya. In a letter he sent to us a few weeks before our visit, Zablon promised to take me to nearby Lake Victoria where we could go looking for hippopotamuses. I was looking forward to doing that until friends in Kenya informed me hippos are roughly the size and speed of Volkswagens and can be violently territorial. Since I'd lost a few steps since my high school track days, I figured we would be better served hanging around Zablon's neighborhood.

We met Zablon at the church where he went to school and spent the day together, thumbing through letters we had sent back and forth for the past ten years. Zablon kept our letters in a spiral-bound book and had arranged them chronologically. Reading those letters and pictures together was like reading through a decade of shared history. And I suppose that's what it was — the process of life, shared together over time.

Meeting Zablon wasn't at all like meeting "a kid in Kenya." This was a bit more like meeting a distant family member. And I know that's how he felt about it because for the six years leading up to our visit, he had signed his letters, "Your son, Zablon." While I found that to be a sweet sentiment, I didn't want it becoming anything more. It was fine and harmless as an idea — I held that idea at arms length like I did with anything having to do with fatherhood.

Zablon pointed to the field adjacent to us and asked Amy, "Would you like to play football?" In the middle of the field was a regulation-sized soccer goal built out of sticks, branches and twine. The director of the program interjected, "He made that soccer goal in expectation of your visit." Zablon knew my wife was a soccer player through letters they exchanged. He then reached into his backpack and said, "I made this as well," holding up a medium-sized ball made out of black plastic bags bound together with multi-colored drinking straws. I remembered there was a leaky faucet in my kitchen I couldn't fix even though I had a box of tools designed to help me do exactly that. Meanwhile, here was this kid making sports equipment out of trash and trees. I decided the very first thing I would do when I got home would be to pick up those tools and move them to the kitchen where I would then pick up the phone to call my friend Jesse to come fix the faucet with the tools I have. A few weeks after we got home, Amy and I received a letter from the Compassion program director in Kisumu, informing us that Zablon's father had died in an accident. We wrote back a short note that took a long time to write because we kept thinking we needed to say something perfect. But simple and clear words usually do the trick. So we wrote: "We love you, Zablon. We are praying for you."

In my recollection, it seems only a few days passed before we were sitting at our kitchen table reading the letter Zablon sent back. I'm certain it was longer, but the timeline around these events in my memory was dislodged by the letter's content, along with almost everything else inside of me. It was a sweet letter, thanking us for our visit and for our prayers. And then, in the middle of the letter, Zablon wrote: *"I was sad that my father had died but I know I have a Father in heaven. Do you know that you, too, are as a father to me?"*

And upon my first reading of the letter, those words *"you . . . are as a father to me"* started ringing in me.

Zablon didn't know that during the flight to visit him, Amy and I talked about whether or not we wanted to have children and I expressed my lack of desire to do so. I wasn't afraid or disenchanted. Nor was I concerned about my ability to correctly pronounce and spell "meconium." I just didn't want to be a father. It wasn't in my heart. But the words of his letter got inside me like a well-crafted melody and they keep ringing. And ringing. And ringing. Like notes ring out in a concert hall. They rang clearly and loudly until my emotional architecture stopped ringing in they key of "I'm sorry, I just can't . . . " and started ringing in the key of "you . . . are as a father to me." The song in me changed. My story changed. My process restarted. I realized I had let my father's story begin to color what I believed about my own, as if the past had some irreversible power over my future. I had almost quit on part of my process in a sadly similar way as my father had quit on his.

But I didn't. Thank God.

On June 5, 2010, Amy gave birth to our son, Asa Jonathan. She became a mother and she is inspiringly good at it. I became a father. I *am* a father. And I want to be. How wonderful are those moments in the process of life when we want exactly what we have. I often find myself completely satisfied just sitting on the floor, watching my son park my wife's old Matchbox cars in a cereal box while he sings, "La, la, la, la, light bulb."

Asa Jonathan's name is a constant reminder that the patterns of depression, workaholism, and self-doubt that marked my father's history have ended with me. I will not live like that. Neither will my son. Asa's presence in my life, my home, my office, or in the pantry where he can often be found stealing crackers out of the box, is the surest evidence I have that change and newness are not only possible but, if I am to believe the promises of Scripture, inevitable.

Like an image in the process of being printed, my life has been incomplete only because it is not over yet. And just like the black ink dots of a printed image are key to that image's clarity and depth, the darkest elements in my process may be key elements but they are only part of it and not the whole.

Which leads me to believe that no moment of my life has been wasted; no failure or success is definitive; no season is absolute; no judgment is conclusive — particularly the judgments I pronounce on myself. So long as there is tomorrow, I have hope for change and newness. Every day, every friendship, every square inch of my life acts like a tiny dot of color making up one small piece of the image of my life. And my life is yet only one small piece of the Grand Image to which every life belongs and finds its place. I believe the Maker of the Grand Image will make it not only true, beautiful, and good, but in the end, very good.

Afterword

From atop the hill adjacent to my home I can see Mt.
Diablo, looming over the valley that bears its name. I've
grown up in its shadow and though I've lived in a few
different places here in the Diablo Valley, I could always see
the mountain from outside my home. Mt. Diablo is just over
sixteen miles from where I live now, and its distance
provides a spectacular perspective. Standing on that adjacent
hill, the mountain appears grey-brown and today I can see
that there is a touch of snow resting about its crest. Yet, as
magnificent as my view is, it is only one way to see and know
the mountain. The things I truly love about the mountain
are things I've learned in the time I've spent on its trails and
along its ridges — a proximity that comes at the cost of
seeing the big picture. Similarly, the things I most value
about the process of life together have generally come into
focus when I stop trying to see the big picture and pay
particular attention to the part right in front of me.

My role as an artist and communicator has afforded me the
opportunity to travel and see the process of life from a
uniquely wide perspective. I've seen heartbreaking poverty
and dizzying wealth. I've seen beautiful acts of love that I
could not capture in words and terrifying acts of injustice
that I simply lack the desire to recount. And as thankful as I
am for this perspective, I am learning that its most vital

function has been to enrich the soil in which my life is rooted, right here in the San Francisco's East Bay Area. The CMYK Project is a fruit of my life as it has been fed by powerful experiences in distant, exotic places like Kisumu City, Calcutta and Cleveland. But most fundamentally, it is a fruit of my life as it has been nourished by my roots — roots that are planted in this particular place and among this particular people. My experiences while traveling have been inspiring and enlightening, and they will continue to be. But it has been my choice to intentionally belong somewhere that has given the richness of those experiences a particular purpose — namely enriching the soil beneath my feet.

If you would like to process something you read or heard in the CMYK Project, don't hesitate to email me: Justin@JustinMcRoberts.com.

You can also find me on Facebook and Twitter.

But it may not be me you are feeling a need to connect with. Instead, it may be the case that, as you read this book, you held the image of a loved one in your mind; someone who needs to hear from you. If so, write a letter to that friend or sister or brother or parent. The words you have for the people you love can only be written or spoken by you.

About the Author

Justin McRoberts is known for the quality and impact of his words. A thoughtful and talented songwriter, storyteller, teacher and advocate, Justin communicates with artistry, humor and honesty. He is one of the founding pastors at Shelter Covenant Church, in San Francisco's East Bay Area where he lives with his wife and son. You can read more from him at his blog: www.justinmcroberts.com

Thanks

Greg Madsen

for your partnership and inexhaustible creativity. Also for your faith in me and for your friendship; I'm glad we get to do this together.

Dan Portnoy

for the way your vision gives me confidence in my own.

David Dark

for your courage to tell the truth, but tell it slant.

Mark Labberton

for your mentorship and encouragement.

Shelter Covenant Church

for being the people with whom I get to live out this process.

Jenni Simmons

for being a kind and generous editor.

Monica Evans & Cathy McRoberts

for your very helpful last-minute proof-reading.

Amy

for making my whole life better.

19706645R00091

Made in the USA
Charleston, SC
07 June 2013